Ethics, social research and consulting with children and young people

Priscilla Alderson and Virginia Morrow

Ethics, social research and consulting with children and young people

Barnardo's 2004
Revised and updated from
Listening to children: children, ethics and social research (1995)

Published by Barnardo's
Tanners Lane
Barkingside
Ilford
Essex
IG6 1QG

Charity registration no 216250

First published 1995 as *Listening to children: children, ethics and social research*
This edition 2004

Designed and produced by Barnardo's Creative Services.

A catalogue record for this book is available from the British Library.

ISBN 1 904659 07 1

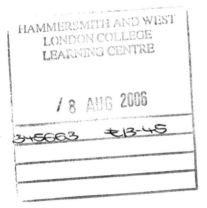

Acknowledgements

We are grateful to Di McNeish and her colleagues at Barnardo's, particularly Helen MacDougall, for helping with the report and for organising a discussion day in March, 2003. We would also like to thank everyone who attended that day from around the UK, and contributed valuable ideas. Helen reviewed ethics guidance about research with children and arranged group discussions with young people on their views about being consulted.

We thank people who sent us ideas, comments and examples, and everyone who has taken part in the recent growth in research and consulting with and by children and young people, on whose reports we have drawn. We regret that we did not have space to include all the contributions. We hope that we have managed to reflect the exciting and varied activities that have taken place since the first version of this report was published in 1995. We hope the report offers some useful ideas for what promises to be further progress on the ethics of consulting with children and young people.

We would like to thank Kate Woodman, Angela Hutton, and two anonymous referees for their helpful comments on earlier drafts of this report.

Views expressed in this report are those of the authors and not necessarily of Barnardo's.

Priscilla Alderson is Professor of Childhood Studies, Social Science Research Unit, Institute of Education, University of London.

Virginia Morrow is Research Lecturer in Child Focused Research, Centre and Department of Health and Social Care at Brunel University.

Contents

Foreword...7

Introduction...9
    0.1   Children's rights..10
    0.2   Newer approaches to consulting and researching directly
           with children and young people..10
    0.3   Research ethics...11
    0.4   The purpose of the report: starting from uncertainty...............11
    0.5   Which investigators, activities and methods does
           this report cover?...13
    0.6   Contents of the report..15

Part 1 The planning stages...*19*
Section 1 – Planning the project: purpose and methods...........................**21**
    1.1   Two basic questions...21
    1.2   Purpose and methods..21
    1.3   Do theories matter?..22
    1.4   Do viewpoints matter?..23
    1.5   Do methods matter?..24
    1.6   Three phases in growing awareness of research ethics...............25
    1.7   Three ethics frameworks for assessing research..........................28
    1.8   Uncertainty – the basis of ethical research..................................32

Section 2 – Assessing harms and benefits..**35**
    2.1   Harms...35
    2.2   Benefits..36
    2.3   Risk, cost, harm and benefit assessments....................................37
    2.4   Confusion in risk-benefit assessments..39
    2.5   Risk of distress or humiliation...40

Section 3 – Respect for rights: privacy and confidentiality....................43

    3.1   Legal rights to confidentiality..43

    3.2   Opt-in or opt-out access..46

    3.3   Practical respect..47

    3.4   Privacy rights, the Data Protection Act 1998........................49

    3.5   Intimacy between strangers...52

    3.6   Rights and the internet..54

    3.7   Does traditional ethics cover modern research

          experiences and relationships? 55

Section 4 – Designing research: selection and participation 59

    4.1   Framing the topics and extent of the research........................59

    4.2   Combining respect, inclusion and protection..........................62

    4.3   Does traditional ethics cover social exclusion?......................64

    4.4   Beyond inclusion to participation..64

Section 5 – Money matters – contracts, funding projects and paying

participants 69

    5.1   Planning and budgeting..69

    5.2   Paying young researchers and participants 71

Section 6 – Reviewing aims and methods: ethics guidance and committees....75

    6.1   Review and revision of research aims and methods................75

    6.2   Does social research need research ethics committees? 76

Part 2 The data collecting stages...81

Section 7 – Information 83

    7.1   Research information leaflets..83

    7.2   Leaflet layout..87

    7.3   Leaflets in other languages...88

    7.4   Two-way information exchanged throughout the project........89

Section 8 – Consent 95
    8.1 The meaning of consent 96
    8.2 Consent and the law 98
    8.3 Consent by and for children and young people 98
    8.4 Complications in parents' consent 100
    8.5 Defining and assessing competence to consent 102
    8.6 Levels of involvement in decision-making 105
    8.7 Requesting and respecting consent and refusal 106
    8.8 Why respect children's consent? 108

Part 3 The reporting and the follow up stages 113
Section 9 – Disseminating and implementing the findings 115
    9.1 Dissemination: getting to the heart of debate and change 115
    9.2 Dissemination and implementation: children, young people
          and adults working together for change 116
    9.3 Problems with dissemination and some potential solutions 118
    9.4 Dissemination and the mass media 121
    9.5 Critical readers and viewers 123

Section 10 – The impact on children 125
    10.1 What collective impact can research have on children? 126
    10.2 Reviewing the impact of research on children 127
    10.3 Positive images 128

Section 11 – Conclusion 131
    11.1 Ways forward for individuals and teams 131
    11.2 Questions that cannot be solved by individuals alone 132
    11.3 The need for social research ethics authorities 132

Appendix 1 – Ten Topics in ethical research 137

Appendix 2 – Project information leaflets 143

References 155

Index 169

Foreword

Listening to children, including children who literally or metaphorically have no voice, is central to recognising and respecting their worth. But researching with children and involving them in decisions does not necessarily place researchers and practitioners on the moral high ground above those who in the bad old days would do research on children, or intervene in their lives without so much as a focus group or questionnaire. While it is likely that making research inclusive of children and young people will strengthen some aspects of the research, we cannot take it for granted that participation in research is always in their interests.

Guidelines on ethics do not give us the answers, but they can lead us to ask the right kinds of questions. It is around a decade since Barnardo's first commissioned Priscilla Alderson to write a book which would provide both discussion and guidance on ethics for those conducting research with children. Since Listening to Children: Children Ethics and Social Research was published in 1995, a good deal has changed for the better in research conduct with children, some of which is directly due to this work. In terms of a direct result for children, the influence of a publication can only be a proxy for a successful intervention in children's lives, but the development of widely accepted guidelines for respectful and inclusive involvement of children in the research process has been a big step forward.

Barnardo's is well placed to have produced this further timely publication, building on what has happened over the last 10 years, and could have done no better than ask Priscilla Alderson and Virginia Morrow to do this. Both authors have outstanding records of researching with children and of working closely with colleagues outside the academy to promote good outcomes for children.

This new publication shows how academics and user groups like Barnardo's can work well together to influence the agenda for children. As well as providing much needed guidance, the authors provide practical examples of doing research with research with children from a whole range of people trying innovative methods, and working hard to make involving children a positive experience. The advantages, both in terms of research excellence and in terms of children's rights, of giving proper thought to the most ethical way of answering research questions will be taken forward by this publication, and by those who use it.

Listening to children, hearing them, and acting on what they say are very different activities. This work will provide us with signposts, while encouraging us to create our own paths.

Helen Roberts, Professor of Child Health,
Child Health Research and Policy Unit
City University, London

Introduction

Many more people are asking children and young people about their views on different aspects of their lives – this is a welcome and widespread change. However, research and consultations with and about children raise ethical questions.[1] This report reviews these questions in the order in which they tend to arise during the stages of a project. We aim to help people to think about the questions posed by their projects and about ways of resolving ethical problems.

We define **social research** broadly, to include any project or process that collects and reports the views and experiences of children and young people. 'Research' and 'projects' are used (to avoid lengthy lists of types of projects) as shorthand for, and to include, consultations, evaluations and participatory projects, which all collect and report data, and can all meet with similar ethical questions.

Social researchers are people of any age who carry out any of these kinds of work. We explain later why we include consultants, evaluators and practitioners as 'researchers' (0.4, 0.5, 1.7). Social researchers may aim to add to knowledge, to evaluate services, to inform and to change policy and practice, and/or to promote children's participation and inclusion.

We usually use the term **participants** for people who are being researched, although this is a contentious word, and sometimes it is more accurate to say 'research subjects'.

We have been asked to use the terms **children and young people** through the report and we agree with this approach. However, it may conflict with another aim: to make the report as short and readable as possible. So we often use 'children' to mean everyone under 18 and we emphasise that we include young children too.

This introduction briefly reviews three recent related changes in views on:
- children's rights
- approaches in research and consulting with children
- research ethics.

Then we look at the purpose of this report, and the importance of starting from uncertainty and asking hard questions. We list the people we have written the report for and outline the contents.

0.1 Children's rights

Respect for children's rights has grown since the United Nations agreed the Convention on the Rights of the Child (UNCRC) in 1989. The Convention has inspired countless new policies and projects around the world. The UK government ratified the UNCRC in 1991, and has to report regularly to the UN on progress in implementing the UNCRC. A key right is article 12: children's rights to express their views on all matters that affect them. Many of the UNCRC's 54 articles are about respecting and including children.

0.2 Newer approaches to consulting and researching directly with children and young people

Children's organisations including Barnardo's have been consulting children and young people about their views for several years.[2] The mid-1990s saw increased funding for research directly with children, by universities and by services for children.[3] The government consultation paper *Every child matters* states that 'Real service improvement is only attainable through involving children and young people and listening to their views'.[4] Many consultations use the same methods as 'social research' – but the people doing them may not think of them as 'social research'.[5] The newer approaches and methods involve:

- gathering children's own views through talking with them, asking them to take photos and make diaries, maps and videos about their daily life, besides involving children and young people as researchers themselves.[6]
- seeing children as highly informed experts on their daily life at home and school,[7] whether in early years centres[8] or when being 'looked after' by a local authority,[9] being on long-term ventilation[10] or being a refugee.[11]

All these approaches raise questions about using ethical, respectful methods and theories when involving children and young people.

0.3 Research ethics

Research ethics is concerned with respecting research participants throughout each project, partly by using agreed standards. Medical researchers gradually developed agreed standards over seven decades, and in Britain they now have a national system of regional and local (LREC) research ethics committees, with websites, forms and guidance, and funds to train members and administer committees. Recent inquiries about serious problems in children's health services[12] helped to prompt new concern about medical ethics, and the government is setting new standards for all research conducted through the health authorities and social services departments.[13] Social researchers now have to agree to observe higher ethical standards in all research with people whom they contact through these services. In time, research with non-service-users – everyone else – may become better regulated, to avoid unfair double standards.[14]

When compared with medical ethics guidance, social research guidance can look rather vague and partial (see section 6). While medical ethics guidance is by no means perfect, and involves different kinds of risk and harm from social research, it offers useful ideas for thinking about and promoting ethics in social research and consultation in general. One aim of this report is to promote more discussion among social researchers about these ideas.

0.4 Purpose of the report: starting from uncertainty

Ethics and research and any consultative processes involve asking and trying to answer hard questions. For this reason, they must start from uncertainty. When testing or evaluating welfare, teaching or psychological interventions, researchers must admit honestly to themselves and to the participants that no one is yet certain how effective each intervention is. They may have to juggle honesty with

Advantages of being experienced 'outsiders'

1. You should be expert in efficient methods of planning and conducting thorough projects, on time and to budget. You may see vital issues that insiders overlook (see 0.4).
2. It may take time to work out the key aims. It is practical to work on questions instead of assumptions, such as asking who might or might not benefit from the project findings and what 'benefit' really means in this context.
3. Access may be slow, but this may help to ensure that you have to inform everyone concerned, ask for their consent, and observe high ethical standards.
4. You should be able to set up good working relations with participants quickly. You do not have a history of either good or poor relations with them, which can be an asset. They relate to you as a researcher, and not also sometimes as a colleague or service provider. Your independence might help people to talk to you more honestly about problems, and to expect you to be fair, open-minded and very careful about confidentiality.
5. You have to spend time talking with people about how they could be involved in the project. This can help them to make informed unpressured decisions and so be committed to their part in the project.
6. If you gain their informed trust and respect, the participants might be willing to accept surprising and even unpopular findings from the project – even if your contract and budget end before you can work with them on applying the findings.

One way to combine these advantages is to have mixed teams of insiders and outsiders, though they will have to allow enough time for careful negotiations throughout the project, to do justice to their very different positions. Another way is to fund more time before and after the main data collecting and reporting stages, in order to support involving participants at every stage including planning the project and implementing recommendations.

We suggest that it is vital that insiders are very clear, to themselves and everyone else concerned, when they are, or are not, 'wearing their research hat'. They could wear a 'researcher' badge, to show the times when more critical, challenging and confidential discussions are invited (see 0.4; 1.5 phase 3; 1.7). To point out this crucial difference and independence, we therefore refer to everyone doing research, consultancy or evaluation of their own or other people's services as 'researchers'.

The activities include designing, funding and commissioning research or consultation projects, and collecting, processing, analysing and reporting data. Later stages of reading, discussing, interpreting, and rejecting or applying research findings also have important ethical aspects. The activities may include:

- evaluations and audits of services
- consultations, and projects that seek users' views
- inspections
- participatory projects
- social research projects
- writing reports for the academic, professional and public press
- writing policy and planning reports, that refer to research findings.

The methods of collecting and reporting information include:

- questionnaire-based surveys
- interviews
- observations
- group discussions
- creative activities such as keeping diaries, taking photos and videos or using drawings or drama
- case studies
- analysing, reviewing and conducting systematic overviews of data reported by other researchers.

0.6 Contents of the report

To help you to find the issues you are interested in, the ten main sections are based on ten topics. These review practical ethical questions raised by social research and consultations from the early planning stages onwards. The issues are summarised in the contents, and the questions that the topics raise are listed in appendix 1: *Ten Topics in Ethical Research*. Section 1 also briefly reviews the meaning, history, theories and practice of ethics in research. We have drawn ideas from national and international ethics guidelines, written for health care research, and for social scientists, teachers and social workers, journalists and market researchers. We suggest that some guidance may be too rigid and narrow, so we raise the following questions.

- What can researchers learn from reflecting about their moral feelings and relationships during their projects? (section 3)
- How can researchers complement traditional approaches in ethics with greater awareness of the interests, rights and abilities of children and other disadvantaged groups? (section 4)
- How do financial and professional pressures, time constraints, stress, and many other daily practicalities affect each research project, and what ethical questions do such pressures raise? Should children and young people be rewarded for taking part in projects? (section 5)
- How does the broader social context, including the values, politics and economics of society, affect research with children? (section 6)
- How does research affect all children, beyond the individual researcher-child relationship? What is the collective impact on children and young people when research influences public and media opinion and professional policies and practices? (section 10)
- How can individual researchers and project teams be supported when they try to resolve controversial questions in their work? Are research ethics committees helpful? (sections 6 and 11)

The report also considers ethics during two stages of research that are often overlooked:

- the initial plans when setting up research teams, and possibly involving participants as partners from the start (section 4)
- the final stages after research reports have been published, of disseminating the findings widely and working to link research into policy and practice (section 9).

Section 11 summarises some practical suggestions for future policy for all concerned with social research with children and young people.

Appendix 1 the **Ten Topics** are set out in an easy-to-photocopy format, for use in teaching and discussion sessions.

Appendix 2 includes a summary leaflet, *Taking part in research: notes for young people,* about the ethical research standards they can expect. Teachers might like to use this section for PHSE and citizenship class discussions. Researchers could adapt it when writing leaflets for and by young people about their projects.

Throughout the text, we have included examples sent to us by researchers and others, or from published work. These examples are intended to show how others have faced – and resolved – various problems, and to help our readers in thinking though some of the issues raised. These examples show how sensitive, transparent and ethical research and consultation can be conducted when ethical questions are clarified and checked, directly and implicitly, with other researchers, reviewers, and with the young participants themselves.

[1]   Morrow and Richards (1996), Thomas and O'Kane (1996).
[2]   See for example Barnardo's, Save the Children Fund, the Children's Society, Childline.
[3]   ESRC.
[4]   Borland et al (2001), Hill (2004).
[5]   Lewis, J (2002).
[6]   Christensen and James (2000), Hill (2004), Kellet et al (2004), Punch (2002), Fraser et al (2004).
[7]   Mayall (2002).
[8]   Miller (1996), Clark and Moss (2001).
[9]   O'Kane (2000).
[10] Noyes (1999).
[11] Candappa (2002).
[12] Redfern (2001), Kennedy (2001).
[13] DoH (2001).
[14] Lewis, J (2002).

Part I

The planning stages

Section 1: Planning the project: purpose and methods

1.1 Two basic questions

Two basic ethical questions arise when any research, evaluation, audit, or other consultation is being planned:
- is this work worth doing?
- can the investigators explain the project clearly enough so that any potential participant can give informed consent or refusal?

These two questions lead on to many sub-questions. This section begins by reviewing the sub-questions raised by various research purposes and methods. We then summarise three stages of growing awareness about research ethics. These are linked to three main ethical frameworks for assessing projects based on ideas about: duties, rights and harms or benefits. The section ends by reviewing the importance of starting from uncertainty.

1.2 Purpose and methods

- Are the project questions worth asking and why?
- Have they already been answered – has previous research on this question been checked in a thorough literature search?
- In whose interests are the questions being asked?
- How well do the research methods fit the aims of the research?
- Do the chosen methods offer the best, or at least the most reasonably efficient, means of answering the questions?
- What are the strengths and limits of the chosen methods?

Is the project worth doing?

Research, consultations and evaluations can be unethical in the sense that they ask the wrong questions, or the methods do not fit the question. The projects may waste time and money, come up with useless answers or, even more dangerously, produce misleading answers that support future misguided and even harmful policies.

1.3 Do theories matter?

Research is often described as being either theoretical or practical, but the division is not quite this clear-cut. Firstly, all projects and questions are grounded in theories, as box 1.1 illustrates. We cannot avoid holding beliefs or theories about what children are and ought to be like. For most of the 20th century, developmental psychology dominated the study of childhood. This model tends to construct children as 'human becomings' rather than fully 'human beings'.[1] It was not until theories about children's incompetence began to be questioned, that research which took more account of children's experiences and capacities began to be funded and conducted.[2] When researchers accept theories of childhood that accept children as real people, more mutually respectful ethical relationships during projects develop.

Box 1.1 Defining terms, thinking about theories: young carers of a disabled family member

How many hours of care have to be given in an average week for a child to count as a 'young carer'? And how does that time differ from the housework and childcare and loving support that children give in so many families that do not have a disabled family member? Theories that see children (and also disabled people) as victims and helpless dependents will produce one set of research questions and conclusions. Theories which view children as problem-solvers and inter-dependent contributors interacting with other family members, will produce quite different results.

1.4 Do viewpoints matter?

Researchers used to believe that they could have a single, objective overview of their topic. But there are always many ways of seeing and understanding children and childhood. The different 'standpoints' that researchers take will alter how children's accounts of themselves are elicited and interpreted. Researchers need to think carefully about the standpoint from which they are studying children, and the ethical implications of that standpoint. For example, are they standing in the position of, and trying to take the viewpoint of, children, or of adults, such as parents, teachers, social workers, tax payers? Newer approaches emphasise respecting children's standpoints and competencies, and making this respect part of the research process. So another ethical and useful way to examine theories, instead of taking them for granted, is to be more aware of standpoints, and of the context, the distribution of power, and whose interests are being served by these theories. See box 1.2.

Box 1.2 Evaluating a school-based behaviour programme
(a hypothetical example)
A school invited a team to evaluate its behaviour programme, run by a specialist company, in which the 12 'most difficult' children in the school and their mothers took part in play and education sessions one morning a week. The team was asked to use a questionnaire to collect the views of the teachers, the parents, and the programme company. The team decided to look at a wider range of views and alternatives as well. They asked all the children in the school what they thought about the effects of the programme, whether they thought there might be better ways to tackle behaviour problems, and how they might spend the budget for the programme. The children were much less likely than the adults to think that the programme worked well. They thought the play sessions and budget should be shared more fairly through the school, and they had positive ideas on how all the children and staff could work together to tackle the

---

behaviour problems, instead of calling on outside help. The answers from different groups highlighted how people tend to speak from their own standpoint and interests. The 12 mothers were afraid to criticise the programme. The company praised it. The teachers liked having one morning a week without their most difficult children. The 200 children in the school wanted to have more play programmes as part of every class's lessons.

1.5 Do methods matter?

Section 3 will examine how all data-collecting methods and sources raise ethical questions about respecting the worth and dignity of every member of the human family.[3] However, certain methods can help to include young children actively and respectfully.[4] See box 1.3 for one such approach.

Box 1.3 The participatory Mosaic Approach
Children aged 3-4 years took photographs, went on tours and made maps while talking with adults (child conferencing), to build up a picture of children's perspectives on their early childhood settings and services. The researchers state that the framework for listening to children is:
- multi-method: recognising the different voices or languages of children
- participatory: treating children as experts and agents in their own lives
- reflexive: including children, practitioners and parents in reflecting on meanings and addressing the question of interpretation
- adaptable: to a variety of early childhood institutions
- focused: on children's lived experiences.

Information is gathered and then pieced together for discussion, reflection and interpretation. The approach can be used for many purposes including looking at lives lived rather than knowledge gained or care received. It can be embedded into practice and used as an evaluative tool in individual reviews, internal audits, childcare audits, changes to the environment, promoting an ongoing dialogue, increasing confidence, developing skills and encouraging children to become more active participants. In using this method, it is important to listen carefully, respect children's privacy and avoid regulating and intruding into their free time[5]

1.6 Three phases in growing awareness of research ethics

This section outlines three phases of growing awareness about ethics in medical research,[6] as a background to social research ethics.

Phase 1. Doing 'good' and feeling good: beneficence and duty
Early medical ethics guidelines were about etiquette, relations with colleagues, and promoting public respect for the profession. Some of these standards benefited patients, but they also benefited the medical profession and its authority and power. In the Hippocratic tradition, from the fifth century BC, doctors assumed they knew what was 'good' for patients (box 1.4).

Box 1.4 Phase 1. Beneficence and duty: the main assumptions
- All true professionals fulfil their duty to benefit service users.
- Standards are ensured by training and expert knowledge.
- To be a professional means to be the best judge of what is good for your service users.

Phase 2. Concern about harm: respect and rights
Confidence in these beliefs was shaken by scandals about harmful research. In particular, Nazi research led lawyers to write the first international guidelines on ethical research, the *Nuremberg Code* (1947). This begins:

> 1. The voluntary consent of the human subject is absolutely essential [the ability] to exercise free power of choice, without the intervention of any element of force, fraud, deceit, duress, over-reaching or other ulterior forms of constraint or coercion.

Based on Anglo-American law, the Code respects personal integrity. Only people who are competent to consent should be asked to take part in research. Children were classed as 'pre-competent', and too vulnerable to be research subjects. Potential research subjects should be given enough information about the risks and hoped-for benefits to enable them to make 'an understanding and enlightened decision' about whether they wish to take part in research (box 1.5).

Box 1.5 Phase 2. Concern about harm: the main assumptions
- Professionals are not always benign.
- Professional expertise and self-regulation are valuable but not sufficient safeguards.
- Ordinary people can understand expert information if it is clearly explained.
- Only the potential research subject can make an 'enlightened' decision about whether to consent to research.
- Human rights must be respected.

Phase 3. Confidence yet caution: balancing harm and benefit
The *Declaration of Helsinki*[7] was the first international code on research to be written by doctors, following public concern about dangerously under-researched medical treatments. The declaration seeks to reassure by beginning with the doctors' expertise, and their mission to 'help suffering humanity'. It only very briefly refers to 'informed

consent', and emphasises doctors' assessments of harms and benefits, of whether research is worthwhile, and of how to safeguard subjects' interests. 'Responsibility for the human subject must always rest with the [medical researcher] and never rest on the subject.'

Slowly, doctors have accepted that they can make mistakes and they have extra ethical duties to patients who take part in research. Unfortunately, examples of children being used as 'guinea pigs' in dangerous medical experiments continue to be reported.[8] Gradually, from the 1970s onward, a new discipline of bioethics, a mixture of law and philosophy, developed.[9] Bioethical ideas have spread into networks of guidelines and research ethics committees (RECs) around the world (box 1.6). RECs stress that researchers must explain their work clearly enough to enable people to make informed unpressured decisions about whether or not to join a research project. This report examines bioethics and comments on its strengths and limitations for social research (see section 6).

A key point of bioethics is that doing research about children is very different from caring for them or teaching them. So, for example teachers or play or youth workers may assume that its research is part of the service. But it is unethical for them to do research with the children and young people they work with, without asking for the children's informed consent (see also 0.6 'investigators'). Formal ethical standards are vital in all projects.

Box 1.6 Phase 3. Confidence yet caution: the main assumptions
- Professionals have unique expertise and observe high standards.
- Professional knowledge must be tested and based on sound research.
- Improved professional regulation can promote ethical standards of research.
- Professionals must inform the people they research, and respect their views and decisions about whether or not to join the project.

We suggest that social research ethics has much to learn from the history of medical ethics and forms of guidance such as *The Declaration of Helsinki*.[10] Some large funders ask social researchers to sign that they will observe the declaration. It includes the requirements that:

- researchers should give full information and request consent
- all research on people should be reviewed by an ethics committee (see section 6)
- research protocols should always state the ethical considerations involved
- reports of 'experimentation' not in accord with the Helsinki principles 'should not be accepted for publication' by journals.

Social research guidelines also respect consent, though their standards vary (section 6).

1.7 Three ethics frameworks for assessing research

Three main working methods or frameworks in professional ethics are based on centuries of philosophical debate about **duty**, **rights**, and **harm and benefit**. Box 1.7 shows how these three approaches differ, and the strengths and limitations of each.

Box 1.7 Summary of three ethical frameworks and questions they pose
Duties (deontology)

The duty-based approach is especially concerned with three main duties: justice, respect and the duty to do no harm. A fourth duty, to benefit, is sometimes included. Questions posed by this approach include:

- Are the aims and methods right and fair?
- Are possible benefits and burdens of research shared fairly?
- Does the research show respect for the autonomy of the participants?

■ Does the research obey the Golden Rule: ie, would the researcher want to be treated as the participants are being treated?

■ Might the research be harmful or useless?

Rights

Questions posed by this approach include whether the researchers respect the participants' rights:

■ to what is so far known to be the best available treatment, care or resources?

■ to protection from harm, neglect and discrimination?

■ to self-determination, such as to give informed consent or refusal?

■ to non-interference and to research that is not too intrusive or restrictive?

Harm/benefit (utilitarianism)

The harm and benefit approach analyses the effects of the research, aiming to minimise harm and increase benefit. Questions posed by this approach include:

■ How can researchers reduce or prevent harm and increase the chance of benefit from their work?

■ How do they decide which are the best outcomes to aim for?

■ Whose interests do they put first, the child's, the parents' or the interests of the research or of society?

■ Might there be harm in not doing the research, or not involving children?

Box 1.8 gives a hypothetical example of applying the three frameworks to research about a support programme for young people. It shows that there can be disagreements within, as well as between, the frameworks.

Box 1.8 Applying the frameworks of duties, rights or harm-benefit
A support programme is planned for young people in the community who are dependent on drugs, are self-harming and sometimes talk about committing suicide. The programme staff differ strongly in their views about whether to offer the new scheme.

Examples of different *duty-based* replies might be:
- we must provide the new extra-support scheme at once and fairly to every young person and keep careful research records
- we must protect everyone from an untested scheme and not test them in order to benefit others
- we must respect the young people by informing them and letting them decide whether to join the research scheme
- we must decide how to choose fairly which ones to offer the limited scheme to.

A *rights-based* reply might be:
- everyone has a right to be in the scheme, or to be protected from the scheme, or to decide whether to join the scheme.

Examples of *harm/benefit-based* replies might be:
- we must decide whether the scheme is worthwhile by weighing the possible benefits to each young person against possible harm caused by the scheme, or the harm caused by not being in the scheme
- we must weigh the risks and hoped-for benefits to young people in the pilot scheme against those to many future young people, who might join the scheme if it works well, or be protected from joining if it does not work
- the risk-benefit balance is so uncertain, only the young people can decide.

Limitations of the three frameworks

1. Ethics does not provide clear, agreed solutions. It is mainly useful as a way of exploring dilemmas to understand them more clearly and deeply. Each person tends to favour one or more frameworks and it helps to understand where they are coming from, to prevent cross-purpose conversations.

2. Each framework has pros and cons. There is often disagreement within and between them and debate about which framework is best. Rights and duties tend to refer back to ancient rules, and the aim to do 'what is right' might sometimes seem harsh or unfair. Harm-benefit analysis looks forward to probable outcomes of the decision. The aim is to do 'what seems best', though this may excuse harm to small groups for the benefit of larger groups.

3. Discussions of ethics can tend to be rather bare and abstract and ignore real complex details in each case.

4. New ways of thinking are needed in the ethics of research with children. Traditional ethics rightly stresses the importance of non-interference and avoiding deliberate harm, but little is said of the harm caused by over-protecting children, silencing them and excluding them from research.

5. The rights of different groups can conflict, such as a) children (or other people) who use services or take part in research b) parents and other adults providing care, public services or research; c) the public which pays for these services (see section 4).

In research about conflicting interests, and unequally held power and resources, there is no neutral or impartial ground. It is therefore useful for researchers to examine where their loyalties lie and to question and try to justify their position.

Despite these limitations, the three frameworks offer useful ways of thinking about potential problems in social research and of preventing or reducing the problems. The frameworks are widely understood and are based on common concepts in daily use. Even young children are keen to talk about justice, rights and being kind and fair, though they may not directly use rights language. Yet the frameworks can also confuse detailed ethical assessments.

1.8 Uncertainty – the basis of ethical research

We noted in the introduction (0.4, 0.5) that research involves asking and trying to answer hard, searching questions. This means that researchers must start from uncertainty when they test interventions, explore users' views, or investigate old and new practices when no one yet really knows the answers. How do people who have worked with children for years step back and begin to ask these difficult questions?

- Is my work really effective?
- Should I use better methods and how do I know which ones are better?
- Do I have the courage to doubt my own certainties?
- Is it fair to worry the children and adults I work with, with these troubling questions?
- How will that affect the confidence that my service users need to have in me?
- Surely being a professional means knowing the answers, not asking these questions? (See box 1.9)

Box 1.9 Risking and learning from uncertainty[11]

A reception teacher decided to research why children whose families came from Bangladesh did less well at her English inner-city school than white working class children. She found that small differences in family life, parenting practices, views on childhood, beliefs about work and play, and stress and illness levels made big differences to the children's adaptations to school and their success or failure there.

Perhaps most important, and certainly more difficult, she looked critically at her own profession. She saw that structures in schools, teachers' good intentions and institutionalised racism led some children to become disaffected and learn how to fail.

Teachers' aims to allow all children to follow their own interests and develop their own learning are inclusive in theory, but Western in practice. Many rules are not taught, but must be learned and worked out by the children.[12] This is easier for

---

children living in Western homes and culture than for others, who have many more boundaries to cross but are least likely to ask for help.

The closing recommendations in the study urge teachers:

- to be alert to children's own ways of seeing and understanding and representing the world to themselves[13]
- to relinquish and transfer some of the power to make decisions about curriculum and pedagogy to parents and children;
- to create more equal, co-operative and rewarding relationships with them.[14]

To raise these questions can involve a change of heart as well as a change of mind. It can make professionals feel anxious and vulnerable while they develop new attitudes towards their own knowledge and status and towards their service users' own views. Researchers have to accept that 'good practice' is informed by research and evaluation that take account of service users' views. Ethical research depends on professional and public education about uncertainty, as well as on the courage honestly to admit uncertainty.

When traditional frameworks of duties, rights and harm-benefit are applied to research designs, the ethical questions raised by research become clearer. However, there are further important questions which often remain hidden, as later sections review.

[1]   Qvortrup et al (1994).
[2]   For reviews see James and Prout (1997), Alderson (2000), Mayall (2002).
[3]   UNCRC (1989) preamble.
[4]   Lancaster and Broadbent (2003).
[5]   Clark and Moss (2001).
[6]   Gillon (1986), Beauchamp and Childress (2000).
[7]   WMA (1964/2000).
[8]   Grodin and Glantz (1994), Nuffield (1999), Sharav (2003).
[9]   Beauchamp and Childress (2000).
[10] WMA (2000).
[11] Brooker (2002).
[12] Ibid: 163.
[13] Ibid: 171.
[14] Ibid: 173-4.

Section 2: Assessing harms and benefits

This section reviews ways of assessing risks, harms, costs and benefits in social research. Assessments are important for two reasons. They enable researchers, reviewers and funders to decide whether the research is worth doing at all, and whether it could be made less risky. And later on these assessments help each person asked to take part to make an informed personal decision. Informed consent is the legal means of transferring responsibility for risk-taking from the researcher to the participant. Consent is only 'informed' if the risks are explained and understood. It is useful to think about harm-benefit during the early stages of planning a project, when it is still fairly easy to redesign the study to reduce risks.

2.1 Harms

When researchers and review committees consider the ethical aspects of a project, they can help to protect children from the abuses of over-research. Over-research might mean having too many children in a project, too many interventions, too much intrusion or too many repeated studies on the same questions. There are also problems of under-research. Under-researched projects might miss out vital questions, or have such a low budget and inadequate time scale, or so few children, that they cannot be finished or reported. A large and very important area of under-research is that many services are not evaluated at all. These services may therefore carry on useless or even harmful work unchecked. For example, types of child-rearing that were once approved are now seen much more critically through the eyes of the children affected.[1] Some evaluations have collected only adults' views and not also children's views. There are also numerous crucial areas where no one has yet systematically investigated children's views and experiences.

'Harm' is often invisible and elusive, complicated by different estimations, different viewpoints – researcher's or child's or carers' –

and differences between short and longer-term outcomes. Medical research can seriously harm people, so the need for ethical controls seems obvious. In contrast, many social researchers see their work as largely benign, or at least harmless. Yet social researchers can intrude into people's lives, and cause them great distress and embarrassment either during the project or afterwards, for example in published reports, videos or television documentaries.

2.2 Benefits

Much social research is intended to improve conditions for young people through its reports and recommendations. It also helps to give information about children's own views and experiences that can change policies and opinions in, for example, British local authority services[2] and hospital care[3] or policies for street children in Asia[4] or Mexico.[5] Yet many researchers point out that reports based upon children's views do not bring about change[6]. Research alone seldom brings real benefits without time and effort being spent on disseminating and implementing the findings (see section 10). In this area, 'insiders' such as youth workers who are evaluating their own work, or people campaigning to keep a service open, tend to have an advantage over 'outsiders' who often lose contact after a project.

Some researchers report direct benefits during a project. For example, interviewees may enjoy having a willing listener. However this is not the purpose of projects when the main aim is to collect data. Simply talking may not feel like a benefit to the person concerned, especially if nothing happens after a project about their problems is completed. Another possible benefit may be in the friendly relationship between the researcher and the child participant. Since research is often about disadvantaged children, is fleeting friendliness really helpful? How do children who may already feel rejected or betrayed react when the friendly researcher departs with the data and makes no further contact? Who benefits in the long term?

We have raised these 'real world' problems to show the importance of researchers being honest and fair about their aims and interests and about likely benefits after the project. For example, researchers should explain that when children describe changes they would like to see, these cannot be promised and may not happen. When the project time and budget are too limited for follow up contact, researchers may need to explain this. Funds permitting, the project team could include or work with a support person, perhaps someone known to the children and young people, to give this ongoing contact. Some researchers telephone a week after a particularly sensitive interview to see if the person would like to talk further or to meet an intermediary.

2.3 Risk, cost, harm and benefit assessments

To prevent harmful or inefficient research, risk-benefit assessments can be made at three levels:
- by the researchers
- by ethics, funding and scientific review committees and advisers
- by the people who are asked to take part in the research, and their carers.

All these groups need to have answers to the questions in box 2.1.

Box 2.1 Information needed to decide on the risks and benefits of a project
- What questions or problems will the project deal with?
- Why do they matter?
- How common and how serious is the problem or lack of the knowledge being researched?
- If methods are being tested or compared:
  – Are they new and/or already widely used?
  – How do they differ?
  – What alternative methods are there?
- Is the need to involve children justified?
- Exactly what will participants be asked to do?
- What direct risks might there be to them?

    – Intrusion?

    – Distress or embarrassment?

    – Loss of the standard teaching or care methods?

    – Risks of new or untested methods?

■ How likely and severe might any risks be?

■ How are risks reduced? For example, by:

    – making police checks on researchers before they can meet children?

    – rehearsing with children ways to say 'no' when they do not want to reply?

    – assuring them that this will be respected and that they will not be questioned about why they refuse?

    – ensuring that children who feel worried or upset about the research can talk to someone about it afterwards if they wish? It can be useful to try to find out gently why young people want to refuse. Does the research seem boring or irrelevant? Could it be improved with their help?

■ How can children contact the researcher if they want to make enquiries or complaints?

■ What are the systems to review complaints and then possibly change the research plans?

■ How much of the participants' time will be needed for the research?

■ What payments, fares and other expenses are covered by the project?

    – How can costs be reclaimed and how soon are they repaid? People often need to be reimbursed at once.

■ How will the project findings be used?

■ What are the planned outcomes?

    – New teaching materials?

    – A report?

    – A film?

    – Who are these outcomes designed for?

    – What effects might they have?

■ Who stands to benefit from the research outcomes in future?

    – What group are they?

- Roughly how many people?
- Do the research participants belong to that group?
- Might the findings benefit them, directly or indirectly?
■ If there are any hoped-for 'benefits' what might they be?

2.4 Confusion in risk-benefit assessments

Benefits Risk-benefit analysis is often confused. It is sometimes summed up in this way: 'You weigh up the benefits the project will bring and the risks it presents. If the benefits are greater than the risks, then it is all right to do the project'. Yet analysis is not that simple, for these reasons.

■ How is benefit defined? Adults' definitions of benefit may differ from children's.
■ Some benefits or harms may only be known in the longer term.
■ There may be short-term advantages but no long-term ones.
■ It may be impossible to show that any benefits derive from the new programme, if many other factors are involved.
■ Benefits from social interventions can be hard to define and assess precisely, such as in changes in attitudes or behaviours.

Risks 'Risk' is a vague word. It covers both *possible* and definite harms, both costs and inconvenience. In contrast 'benefits' implies that there will be definite good. So 'risk-benefit' is a loaded phrase. 'Risks and hoped-for benefits' is a more balanced phrase and is more honest about the uncertainty underlying all research.

Risk to a few people taking part in projects on, for example, methods of maths teaching or of foster care, may be balanced against hoped-for benefit to countless young people in future. However, the danger is that researchers can justify any research by claiming huge hoped-for benefits. They need to be clear whether they are considering risk and benefit to each research participant, or are using the much looser equation of risk to the participant and hoped-for benefits to society. *Helsinki*[7] and other codes repeat that the researcher's first concern must be the effects on the individual research subject, although some guidance is vague about individual risks versus collective benefit (see also boxes 1.7. 1.8).

Probability: how likely is the harm to occur? To a certain extent, risk probability can be calculated. The risk of being run over if you cross a road can be worked out from the current average rates. But this is a very vague measure, because so much depends on the type of person and road. Some ethics guidance counts the traffic accident injury rate as an 'everyday risk' in the dubious belief that people will accept similar levels of risk in research as 'minimal'.[8]

Severity: how serious might the harm be? Risk severity cannot really be measured because so much depends on each person's values. For one child, it might be fine to talk on television about crime in her area. Another child might be terrified for months afterwards that she will be picked on and attacked by local criminals. Probability and severity of harm are often discussed as if they are the same thing, whereas they are very different.

2.5 Risk of distress or humiliation

Risks in social research and consultation include distress and anxiety, embarrassment and loss of self-esteem. If researchers are to explain risks, and how probable and severe these might be, they need to listen to children's views on which risks worry them most. Some risks might not occur to researchers. A simple question, such as asking children if they would like to take part in a research project in groups or pairs with their friends, could upset children who feel they have no friends. Other typical harms caused by social research and consultations, such as inconvenience, time lost, intrusion and mental discomfort, may seem slight, but they could be very serious to the person concerned. People can feel wronged by research, if they feel they have been treated as objects, deceived or humiliated, or that their values or privacy have been disregarded. Research ethics is intended to prevent such problems.

[1] Bradley (1989), Cooter (1992), Stainton-Rogers and Stainton-Rogers (1992), Grodin and Glantz (1994).
[2] Willow (1997).
[3] Oswin (1971), Robertson and Robertson (1989).
[4] Karkara and O'Kane (2002).
[5] Liebel (2004).
[6] Donnelly (2003).
[7] WMA (2000).
[8] Nicholson (1986).

Section 3: Respect for rights: privacy and confidentiality

Privacy is a vital ethical concern although it has not always been respected in research with adults or children. This section reviews children's rights to:

■ privacy – avoiding undue intrusion into their personal affairs
■ confidentiality – concealing their identity and sometimes other details when reporting them.

This section reviews legal rights and reports a recent Australian court case on confidentiality. It compares opt-in and opt-out access methods, gives a detailed checklist about respecting privacy and looks at the Data Protection Act, recommending good practice in protecting confidentiality. This section also considers extra questions about privacy raised by intimacy between strangers during research interviews, and in projects that involve emails and websites. Finally, it asks whether duties, rights and utilities (box 1.6) need to be complemented with greater concern about complicated relationships, detailed practices and emotions in research.

3.1 Legal rights to confidentiality

Children have many of the same rights to confidentiality that adults have. For example, competent children can ask their doctors not to inform anyone else about their case and can expect this request to be respected.[1] Children have some extra rights – for example the right not to have their names published in the media if they are involved in the law courts (although this has changed for persistent young offenders). No one has an absolute right to confidentiality and a breach may be justified in rare cases, if it is thought that someone is in serious danger. If so, the researcher should first encourage the person who knows about the danger to talk to adults who could help or else to agree that the researcher should talk to them. 'Guarantees of confidentiality and anonymity given to research participants must be honoured, unless there are clear and overriding reasons to do otherwise, for example in relation to the abuse of children'.[2] The BSA Guidelines also state: 'Research involving children requires particular care.... Specialist advice and expertise should be sought where relevant', although the guidelines do not say where these should be sought.

There are two key ethical questions:
- If it seems necessary to breach confidentiality, is this first clearly discussed with research participants?
- Should participants be warned in advance about the limits of confidentiality?

It is often said that researchers cannot promise confidentiality to children, in case children describe abuse or other information that must be reported, and perhaps demanded, by the courts. A recent case in Australia shows that this is not always so. The case is important in Britain, through the network of Commonwealth Law.

Box 3.1 Research and promises of confidentiality to children: a legal challenge

By Patrick Parkinson Professor of Law and Judy Cashmore Research Psychologist, University of Sydney 2002

A decision of the Family Court of Australia indicated that research conducted with children under express promises of confidentiality may be protected from subpoena (a court order to produce the data). The case (*T v L*, unreported, 12.10.2001, Collier J, Parramatta) arose from research we conducted on children's participation in making decisions about residence and contact following their parents' separation. Parents and children were interviewed only after proceedings were thought to be completed. They were all given express, explicit undertakings of confidentiality, orally and in papers mailed to families by the Family Court of Australia inviting them to contact us.

Dr Cashmore interviewed Mr T and his children, with assurance that no further legal proceedings were contemplated

---

and no subpoenas would be sought. Later, proceedings flared up again. Mr T issued a subpoena seeking Dr Cashmore's notes and interview recordings. He said that he did not want to breach confidentiality but to have some overview of what the children said, and to gain the benefit of Dr Cashmore's impressions, in case these could help the Court. We resisted the subpoena.

Collier J struck down the subpoena on three grounds. First on public policy, noting that all the consents were given with acknowledgment of confidentiality. If projects of this kind 'are to be encouraged, then it is essential that people who wish to take part in these programs know that there is confidentiality. [Also] it is of vital importance that the researchers know that... the confidentiality that they have set up as the basis of those interviews and the whole of their research cannot be impinged upon by the use of a subpoena...such as the present case. I would be satisfied, and find, that on the public policy aspect alone, the subpoena should be struck down.'

Second, on estoppel (prevention) and/or waiver the judge cited a case when an injured naval sailor sued the Commonwealth. The claim would have been barred by the Statute of Limitations, but the Minister gave written assurances that the Statute would not be pleaded. Yet later, the Commonwealth amended its defence, denying the claim and pleading the Statute. High Court Judges held that the Commonwealth was estopped from pleading the limitation period, because it has earlier waived its right to do so. In the same way, Mr T could not change his mind and to say, "Well, yes, I said it could be confidential then, but I no longer say it."

Third, there was a lack of legitimate forensic purpose. This was a 'fishing expedition' to subpoena material in case something came out of it. The judge also noted that the interviews were conducted for research purposes, not as an assessment for court purposes.

Rulings in Australian courts influence case law in other Commonwealth countries. The judgement, albeit given extempore in the course of a trial, suggests that courts will protect bona fide research undertaken with express undertakings of confidentiality. The three grounds were independent grounds, any of which was sufficient to justify striking down the subpoena. The decision should give confidence to researchers in future, who conduct research involving families in conflict.

3.2   Opt-in or opt-out access

Opt-in research can be more respectful of people's privacy than opt-out. With opt-in research, researchers send letters, often via a third person, inviting people to telephone or return a card if they want to take part in the research or to have more details. The researchers may then only know details about people who reply. However this can create barriers that make it harder for researchers to contact certain groups and to include their views. Opt-out research – when researchers phone or knock on doors or send a letter saying that unless the person cancels the visit a researcher will call – gets higher return rates but can invade privacy. Box 3.2 describes one solution to these problems, which readers may like to debate.

Box 3.2 Opt in or opt out by seldom heard groups?
Ruth Marchant, Triangle, reported on research with looked-after young people.

Opt-out research forms sent to young people do not reach them all, such as those who have had recent care placement moves. If they do not return opt-out forms, they are contacted by researchers without their agreement. But opt-in methods can involve losing many people who might like to take part but who do not contact the researchers as requested. Researchers at the National Children's Bureau found that some parents/carers reported that young people were not interested in joining a research project, but the researchers were not always convinced, and sometimes learned that this was not so. Some social workers refused to pass information on to people with sensory, learning or language difficulties, worried that they were not competent to consent or refuse, even when researchers had made extra efforts – modifying participation requests and research methods, and involving translators/signers.

Some recruitment methods discriminate against hard to recruit groups, whose voice needs to be heard and hardly ever is. To research with 30 families, we ask Social Services for, say, 90 names and addresses. Social Services then send families a letter saying that, unless they indicate otherwise, their details will be sent to the research team. We then select 30 names and social services do not know which 30 they are. We send an information pack and letter saying that unless the parents indicate otherwise, a researcher will ring the parent or child at home. A senior researcher will then ring the parents. They rarely refuse despite being traditionally 'hard to reach' families. We usually achieve 98 per cent inclusion of children or families, whereas an earlier project involved only 10 per cent.

3.3 Practical respect

This section looks at respect in a range of methods.
- For example, in the use of records, case notes, archives and other data, when the people recorded are not approached directly, would they mind how their data are used and interpreted?
- Should they be contacted and asked for their consent?
- With questionnaires, how far is it right to ask questions that might offend or upset people? Do questionnaires and highly structured interviews miss out topics, questions and optional replies that participants would consider vital, or that would help to make sense of their seemingly illogical replies or behaviour? Some young people, for instance, might give logical reasons for missing school.
- Do the questions and approaches respect each age group, without talking down to younger children?[3]

Tape recordings, videos and photograph collections raise extra questions about confidentiality.

When collecting children's drawings, maps and diaries, who should have copyright and should their authorship be acknowledged? (See box 7.3.[4])

■ Interviews range from highly structured question-and-answer sessions to informal conversations. As with focus groups and other group activities, do the researchers exert too much control, in ways that make the participants uneasy, or feel made to say more or less than they wish to?

The following list gives some reminders to consider about respect for privacy and confidentiality.

■ How and why have people been chosen? If their names are on confidential lists, such as at risk registers, will researchers ensure that they do not see the lists? Only professionals with access to the list should select the names and approach the people. If the people agree, the researchers can then be informed. Are the people told about means of access to their names and why they were chosen?

■ Is everyone given a choice about whether they are tape-recorded or whether notes are made instead?

■ How will the data – notes, audio or video tapes – be stored so as to comply with the current Data Protection Act? (see section 3.4).

■ Are interviews held in a quiet private place (this can be hard to arrange in homes and schools)? Can interviewees choose for someone else to be present if they wish?

■ Are participants told that everything they say will remain confidential (private) and only quoted when they cannot be identified?

■ Do the participants want this confidentiality? Would they rather be named and acknowledged? If so, what is the best response?

■ Are they warned about limits to confidentiality if they mention serious risk of harm to themselves or to others?

■ In research that uses group discussions how is confidentiality for the people in the group, and the people they talk about, respected? This partly depends on the questions being asked – group discussions are not so useful for disclosing intimate information, but very useful for sharing views, for example, about a local neighbourhood. 'Chatham House rules' can be explained clearly, even to young children. They mean that: 'After the group meeting, you can talk to other people about what we said. But please do not tell them the name of the person who said it, or the names of any people they were talking about.'

■ If other people apart from the research team will be informed about the research sessions, do the participants know and agree to these named other people being informed?

■ Who will see research records, transcripts, notes, tapes or films? Some journal editors now ask researchers to request consent from everyone whose photograph they wish to publish in research reports.

■ Will research participants have a copy of any relevant letters to other people, such as if researchers write to teachers, psychologists or social workers about a child?

■ How will reports be published in ways that protect privacy (change of names and other details?)

■ Is consent to more public reports and other use of data such as photographs or videos specifically requested from each person?

■ Do the research participants have any kind of editorial control, such as being able to ask for some comments they have made to be omitted from any reports, and to check for fairness and accuracy?

■ Are participants asked to agree to any follow up research, or secondary use of their data such as through data archiving? The ESRC, for example, wants projects to be archived, potentially for other researchers to use. When is it best to ask people for their extra consent to this? You do not want to overwhelm them with complicated requests before an interview, but is it good enough to ask them later in the project? Or is it better to ask them later, when they know much more about what they have said, and how they might like it to be used or not used?

3.4   Privacy rights

Ethics emphasises respect, rights and equality, whereas most services for children emphasise protection. The meaning of rights has expanded from the early rights to respect for autonomy, non-interference and privacy, to include *provision* rights to certain resources, such as education and health care, and rights to *protection from harm*[5] (although protection was included in the early ideas about autonomy[6]). However, provision and protection stretch the meaning of 'rights' from the original idea of non-interference, into active interference, albeit in the child's interests. While protection is important, over-protection can lead to children being treated as passive objects of concern, rather than as active moral agents in their own right[7], and this can expose them to greater risk of being exploited and even abused by researchers.[8] Explicit rights, such as those spelt out in the 1998 Data Protection Act, can help to clarify areas of conflict, and regulate relations between participants and researchers.

The Data Protection Act 1998

Each fairly large research institution has an officer to advise on data protection and to register projects under the Act. People working on projects in small agencies also need to check details of the Act and register their projects. This includes keeping full details on:

- purposes for holding the data
- sources of the data
- individuals and organisations to whom data are disclosed
- the sorts of data you hold
- whether you hold particularly sensitive data, such as ethnic origin
- whether you intend to transfer data abroad.

Box 3.3 Some key points from the Act
- Personal data are any data about a person (data subject) that can be used to identify that individual.
- Data must be obtained and processed fairly and lawfully.
- Individuals who supply data must be made fully aware of why they are asked to do so.
- Data must be held and used only for the specified, agreed purposes.

- Data must not be disclosed to any person or organisation other than ones mentioned when the data are collected.
- Data should be adequate, relevant and not excessive to the purpose for which they are held.
- If there is no planned use for them, data should not be kept.
- Data must be accurate and kept up to date.
- Personal data must not be held longer than is necessary. Data should be erased when there is no further use for them.

Individuals must be allowed access to any data held on them, including paper records. A printout must be produced within 40 days, including photocopies of all paper documents held on the individual. Institutions may be fined if they do not comply. This does not apply to research records, provided data are published in a purely anonymous statistical form and no data are disclosed that would help to identify an individual. If any sort of identification is published, then the data are no longer anonymous and data subjects then have access rights. (In small qualitative studies, people may be quite easily identified, even when they are anonymous. It is wise to keep very careful, respectful records, in case the people concerned ever wish to see them.)

Good practice on confidentiality
- Take reasonable measures to ensure that unauthorised people cannot access the data in computer and paper records. If personal data are displayed on a screen, log out before leaving the office, even for a short while.
- During a project, if you need to collect more, or less, or different data, or to disclose data to different people, you must alter your registration records.
- Take extra care with sensitive personal data, such as data about racial or ethnic origins, political opinions, religious beliefs, physical and mental health, sexual orientation or habits and criminal convictions.
- Only hold sensitive data if you have explained to the data subject why you are using the data, and the data subject has consented.

- All personal data must be handled with appropriate safeguards for the rights and freedoms of the data subject.
- If you save word processing documents with letters and other documents that contain names and addresses and other identifiable details, you must register them. (It is better to anonymise all computer and other records, and to keep them separate from records of personal details.)

Respect for privacy rights at home Parents or carers may want to join in young people's interviews at home. As 'guests' of the family, interviewers cannot easily request a private space for candid interviews or use the privacy of the child's bedrooms, for child protection reasons. Some children may prefer to be interviewed with their parents, at least for the first part of their session, and families' choices and interactions can provide very useful insights. Some parents help their children to give fuller replies. However, other parents may inhibit and irritate their children. If so, researchers may have to try tactfully to arrange a follow up in another setting.

Confidentiality or acknowledgement?
Sometimes, children want to be recognised for the research data they give and for their views and experiences, their drawings or maps. Yet if children are named, they may be identifiable. And if one child is identified, others in their group or school who do not wish to be identifiable may become so. These questions need to be discussed so that reasonably fair solutions may be agreed.

3.5 Intimacy between strangers

Research interviews Ethics pervades every step of research. For example, the aim of interviews is to set up mutual respect, trust and rapport quickly, to obtain personal and sometimes intimate and distressing details. There is an odd balance between businesslike and friendly relations. This involves interviewers using sympathetic techniques:
- sitting at the same eye level, not too close or too distant, in a quiet, comfortable, private place

- asking for permission to make notes or tape recordings
- letting children hear their own voice on the tape if they wish
- encouraging them by talking clearly, fairly slowly and not too loudly, keeping eye contact, looking and sounding interested.

Some people may agree to be interviewed but seem very unwilling or bored, shy or embarrassed during the interview. Some do open up with gentle prompting. If they do not, researchers could try further topics. If these do not improve matters, it is respectful to talk for a while and then end the interview positively and thank them without suggesting it may have been a waste of time.

Some children like to have a copy of their transcript or tape but before offering these it is worth thinking about how confidential these might remain. The children might have said things about family members who might find the transcript.

Group sessions can also be arranged like a meeting between friends, with chairs in a close circle, and simple requests such as 'please don't interrupt', 'listen to what each person says' and 'please talk clearly for the tape recorder'. Children should be able to feel free to have a break, pause, and say, 'I don't want to talk about that', or 'let's stop now'. Many researchers recognise that children may be more comfortable in pairs or groups and often prefer to choose how they wish to take part.

These interactions can feel genuine to the researcher, although they do involve skilled techniques and there is an imbalance between the data-giving by participants, and the data control by researchers. However, rapport is complicated during interviews by the authority that adults hold over children. Assurance that 'you can tell me any time you want to stop' tends to deny powerful influences that may deter interviewees from saying they want to leave.

Researchers should be sensitive to children's reluctance, which they may be unwilling to express. People can be distressed by being asked sensitive questions about, for example, bullying, being disabled or living in a family with HIV. Even simple topics might very much distress people; pets, for instance, if their dog has just died and they are not ready to talk about it. Children should be assured from the start that it is their right to withdraw at any stage, stop an interview or not answer a question. This can be rehearsed before the interview. Researchers should be alert to signs of distress or reluctance. Road traffic style signs help children to show if they want to stop or withdraw (they can hold up the red disc), pause (the amber disc) or continue (the green disc).[9] If respect for young participants is genuine, it is honoured through all stages of the project, in efforts to collect, understand and present their views as fairly as possible.

3.6 Rights and the internet

New technologies bring people into very close contact across the world. In a European project, young refugees joined local e-groups and also an inter-European network. The project had to develop ways to support private exchanges through the closed local groups and also more anonymous guarded contact when groups contacted one another through more public systems.

British Sociological Association ethics guidelines urge caution. Members should take special care when researching via the internet. Ethical standards for internet research are not well developed yet, and eliciting informed consent, negotiating access agreements, assessing the boundaries between the public and the private, and ensuring the security of data transmissions all raise problems. People who do research online are advised to ensure that they know about ongoing debates on the ethics of internet research, and to be careful about respecting the well-being and privacy of online research participants. Online direct consultations also raise these issues in this fast changing field (box 3.4).

Box 3.4 Advantages and disadvantages of online consultations

Advantages
- Children and young people often enjoy this method of communication and see it as relevant.
- It can yield candid information about children's views and priorities.

- It works well together with other methods of consulting, either to supplement other methods or to glean initial views at the planning stage.
- It can provide wide and cheap access to the views of children and young people.
- It can help to reduce social inequalities when disadvantaged children are involved, for example, via their schools.

Disadvantages:
- It does not necessarily provide a representative group of children and young people, and a few people may give many replies under different names.
- Many children and young people do not have access to computers.
- It is very hard to gauge anything about the characteristics of the children who are commenting – some may be adults in disguise.
- If accessed through school, children's responses may be influenced by teachers.[10]

3.7 Does traditional ethics cover modern research experiences and relationships?

Section 1.6 outlined how traditional ethics concerned duties, rights and utilities or harms/benefits. These tend to be impersonal approaches, not interested in emotions and implying that research runs smoothly as long as it is well planned and managed. In practice, many problems and dilemmas arise throughout projects, especially in sensitive topics with children and other vulnerable groups. If social research ethics is to review complex details seriously, it has to take greater account of relationships, power and emotions (boxes 3.5-3.6).

Box 3.5 Research relationships and power
- How do researchers' skills, in listening, talking and sharing knowledge and decisions with children affect how they work with children as partners and learn from them?
- How do these skills affect the way researchers evaluate interventions and their own work, and try to raise standards?
- How do researchers try to take account of power differences between adults and children, researchers and participants, service providers and users?
- How do they try to avoid the misuse of power and to respect children's rights and interests?
- How do they know the children's views on their own best interests?

Box 3.6 Emotions
- How do researchers try to be aware of their own feelings, their hopes for their research, fear and anxiety about mistakes, or worry about lack of time and resources and about stress, uncertainty and failure?
- How do they try to learn from, and act on, these feelings?
- How do they respond to children's and adults' distress or anger?
- How do researchers celebrate positive aspects of their work?

The role of emotions in research is debated. Do emotions bring new insights or cloud judgement? Does emotion lead researchers to become over-involved? There are advantages when researchers identify emotionally with their participants, while still respecting and exploring personal differences.[11]

In stressful and sensitive topics, there is perhaps an ethical requirement that research teams provide support and debriefing for researchers. With researchers' agreement, this can be a valuable resource both to support individual researchers, and to inform the research processes and findings by the insights gained through feelings.

Besides the rather inward-looking practicalities concerned with emotions in boxes 3.5-3.6, ethical research also looks outwards to larger political concerns, considered in the next section.

[1] Montgomery (1997): 301.
[2] BSA (2002): Clause 37.
[3] Solberg (1997).
[4] See also Kellett and Nind (2001), Lewis, A (2002).
[5] Franklin (2002).
[6] Plant (1992).
[7] Kessel (1989).
[8] Cooter (1992), Sharav (2003).
[9] Example sent by National Children's Bureau.
[10] Borland et al (2001).
[11] Woodhead and Faulkner (2000).

Section 4: Designing research: selection and participation

Selecting samples or groups to research is one of the first tasks in a project. New moves to include children work well where the ethics, methods, including sample selection, topics and outcomes of the research all reinforce one another and are not contradictory. This section reviews the pros and cons of different framing and selection criteria. Traditional ethics tends to take a liberal position, as if all people are equal, but this can sidestep politics, economics, social exclusion and inequalities and the ethical problems they raise. Examples of social research with children from around the world show how research ethics can take a broader view of justice.

4.1 Framing the topics and extent of the research

Every project has to exclude many issues in order to concentrate on specific questions and topics and arrive at definite conclusions. Deciding how wide a research area will be may seem like positioning a camera lens and choosing what will be inside and outside the frame of the photograph. But social research has also to take some account of the broad context, both inside and outside the frame, both around and central to the participants. There are no clear cut-off lines.

For example, research on school truants might simply record days absent. But understanding truancy involves researching the truants' views and motives, and their experiences inside and outside school. This might lead to examining different school policies and budgets to explain variations between schools, and between factors such as family income, ethnicity, or health, or local employment opportunities. Box 4.1 shows how listening to young people brought vital findings into a project on exclusion.

Box 4.1 Extra exclusions

Although 17 per cent of students officially excluded from school are girls, they tend to be ignored. Girls feel that teachers set double standards, overlook subtle bullying among girls and girls' subdued depression, and intervene more to help boys. Help for girls is often poorly co-ordinated, especially when they are carers at home, are pregnant and have their own children. Many girls opt out and 'self-exclude'. Unofficial and unrecorded exclusions are more likely to happen to girls than to boys. In vital ways, girls suffer extra problems that leave them even more unseen, unnoticed and excluded.[1]

This kind of broader, more inclusive research can produce clearer analyses. It can also be more fair and ethical to take account of the wider context, rather than assuming that the problem lies wholly with the individual child or young person or the parents. The broad or narrow framing of research relates to ethics and justice as well as to methods.

Pros and cons of exclusions criteria: research with children last?
Children are among the groups that have been most excluded from research. Medical ethics guidelines, in many ways rightly, say, 'Research which could equally well be done with adults should not be done with children'.[2] Women who might be pregnant are also often excluded. Yet as a result, most medicines are tested on men aged 16-60 years, and little is known about the doses that children need and the reactions they may have. This medical example illustrates similar problems in other areas – education, play, social and voluntary services. When children's unique and valuable views are unknown because of lack of research – as overviews about research on children's diet and exercise show[3] – it is harder to ensure that the best services are provided or that harmful services are changed.

There are important protective reasons for excluding children from projects:

■ adults tend to have more experience to alert them to risks in research

- adults have more confidence and independence to enable them to refuse or withdraw if they wish to
- adults may have more resilience and be less likely to be hurt by the research
- researchers are likely to take an adult's wish to refuse or to withdraw more seriously.

However, instead of emphasising children's supposed vulnerabilities, our report is concerned with how to design and promote ethical lower-risk research with and for children and young people.

Box 4.2 Equal opportunities[5]
The group Children in Scotland is committed to equal opportunities and believes that all children are of equal worth, whatever their ability, colour, ethnicity, gender, health, religion, sexual orientation or social class. These principles must be carried through into research design and conduct within the limits of available resources.
To promote inclusive practice, Children in Scotland will:
- where possible, invite interested parties (including children and minority groups) to participate in defining the aims, design and key concepts of a study before it begins
- avoid the use of exclusionary language in research proposals
- within the limits of resources adapt or adopt particular techniques to ensure all those eligible can participate equally regardless of ability or literacy
- avoid condoning or perpetuating prejudice and stereotypes in the research that is proposed or conducted.
The guidance adds that: recruitment must recognise diversity and use non-exclusionary methods.

Projects often protectively exclude children who speak little English, or who have learning or speech difficulties. These projects therefore are likely to produce incomplete and misleading findings. The opposite ethical approach is to make every process throughout the project as inclusive as possible. Then project methods can reinforce the conclusions that inclusion is possible and can work very well. (See box 4.2, and the Diversity and Difference Group project in section 9.)[4]

Some disadvantaged groups, such as families with multiple problems, risk being over-included if they are asked to take part in too many research projects. Alternatively, they may be among the least consulted people and the least involved in planning projects. This is another area where ethics committee review (section 6) can help, to ensure that the benefits and burdens of research are fairly shared.

4.2 Combining respect, inclusion and protection

Ethics involves finding a balance between unwanted extremes. One researcher considers this in these terms:[6]

> How do you get a balance between giving young people an opportunity to voice their opinions while ensuring we meet the highest ethical standards for such research? We sought permission from the local authority and talked to all the immediate carers. Carers were invited to ring if they had any further concerns, and they received a letter from their local authority. In many cases, social workers were also contacted. Although we did not contact parents (ideally this should have happened but many young people were in long term care and I think would not have wanted us to approach their families) my starting point was that of a parent. I would want to know to whom my children were talking, what about, and I would want to ensure that my children were safe in their hands. Great care was taken with the venue, transport and other arrangements. Built into our research plan were agreements with the local authorities about what we would do should a young person disclose information which suggested that he or she was at risk of significant harm. All young people were 'invited' to take part, and the decision about whether to join the group or not was theirs. There were three sessions and if a young person did not wish to join all the sessions that was up to them. Very few dropped out.

After describing more measures to respect choice and confidentiality, she added:

> However, I do worry that these guidelines might be used to block young people's access to reputable researchers. In our study, young people had to sign a letter and return it to us if they wished to be involved. Some of the young people appeared to be deliberately diverted from taking part, because for example they were all taken out swimming. It is very difficult for young people who are being looked after to voice their opinions in safe forums. One young man was so keen to attend that he walked three miles to the meetings on three occasions. Again and again, the young people told us how much they appreciated the chance to talk in the groups. They asked for more such groups to be set up around the country. I do worry that too tight ethical guidelines might be used to shut the door on what young people have to tell us. That would be a retrograde step.

People who review and assess projects might ask:
- Is it clear why children need to be involved?
- Is it clear why children are excluded, and have they been asked to consent to being discussed and reported about by adults?
- Are parents encouraged to stay with children during research sessions, if the children wish this? Young children can be more scared about being left with strangers than about research interventions.
- Are efforts made to speak to children separately if they wish to, to help them to express independent views?

Researchers protect children and themselves when they are able to discuss the problems with colleagues, advisers and reviewers, and when they justify their decisions in their research reports (and see section 6).

4.3 Does traditional ethics cover social exclusion?

Traditional ethics tends to see society as fair and equal, working well to benefit every social group. A more critical view sees different groups as competing for power and resources, and sometimes harming one another. If social research ethics is to review inequalities and exclusions seriously, it has to take account of unequal and unjust social structures beyond traditional views of duties and utilities.

4.4 Beyond inclusion to participation: children and young people as researchers

Children are increasingly involved as researchers.[7] Concern about inequalities and inclusion has led researchers and others to work especially with – not just for – disadvantaged children and young people to develop participatory approaches and techniques. Many reports and handbooks record participatory methods and projects,[8] such as with street children in South America[9] and children's clubs in South Asia.[10] See box 4.3.

Box 4.3 Projects organised by young researchers from start to finish
Seven British children aged 9-10 years worked with an Open University lecturer in a weekly research club during their lunch hour at school. They spent 10 weeks learning how to do research, then they chose their topics and conducted their own projects. Their research reports set out their questions, methods, findings, discussion, and conclusions ending with a section 'if we could do this project over again we would...' One report begins, for example:

'We were interested in how parents' jobs affect their children and wondered how children are affected by the kind of hours parents work and the sorts of moods they come home in, for instance if they come home very tired or angry or if they come home happy and bouncy. How does this affect the quality of relationships in the family? We also wondered how many parents

---

worked and how long their hours were. We wanted to investigate this from children's viewpoints, not adults'. The research question we decided on was: 'how are children affected by the nature of their parents' work?' We predicted that most children would prefer their parents to work shorter hours and be able to come to watch them in more school events. What we found out surprised us.'

The reports show how highly competent young researchers can be.[11]

In Kenya, children with HIV/AIDS were involved in researching, planning, implementing, monitoring and evaluating services for themselves and their peers. The ethical participatory methods helped to make services more effective, guided by UNCRC principles. The project workers reported that the children needed little training apart from information about the processes and purposes of the projects. The main training, they said, was for the adults, to help them to overcome their misunderstandings and mistrust of children and to learn to work with them more equally.[12]

However, participatory approaches involve the same challenges and problems as other research. Much time and care are needed to train and support the researchers. There may be power, age, ability, ethnic and gender inequalities between the children and young people involved, as well as between them and the adults. Participatory and emancipatory research seldom has practical outcomes unless these are planned and worked for throughout the whole project.[13]

Children and young people themselves are well aware of inequalities, as these girls, who discussed whether there was a new local youth forum, showed:[14]

> Gemma: No-one knows about it, if there is one.
> Tamisha: I think there should be one, but...
> Miranda (interrupting): But they'd choose the people who do all the best in school and everything, and they're not average people, are they?

In some ways during participatory projects, the risks of exploiting children increase. Extreme care is needed to avoid unethical pressures on individuals and groups. The handbooks and reports noted above include many practical ideas about working with young people on their own terms, and using young advisory groups to help to prevent and deal with problems.

It is also vital to remind children and adults that research itself does not bring change. Children and young people are eager to know what will change as a result of their research or consultation. The more they have invested, the greater their disappointment and perhaps disillusion could be if nothing is achieved.

Authorities may simply ignore even high quality reports. Or the research may not provide strong enough findings to support a cause that the project was designed to promote. Even if some people are convinced by the data, critics might not be. Much extra hard work is usually needed, for a long period after the research project is completed, if policy makers and practitioners are to learn about the findings, accept, and possibly implement them (sections 9 and 10).[15] By then, the young people may be much older and have moved on before any effects can benefit them.

When research ethics includes a broader social and political analysis, the rights, duties and harm/benefit frameworks can be enlarged to gain a richer understanding of the research topics, context, methods and the impact of research on children, as reviewed in following sections.

1. Osler et al (2002).
2. RCPCH (2000).
3. Brunton et al (2003).
4. See also Ward (1997), Morris (1998), Noyes (1999), Lewis, A (2002) Cleves School (1999).
5. Children in Scotland (2002).
6. Anonymous researcher in Alderson (1995):42-3.
7. France (2000), Alderson (2000) Kellett et al (2004).
8. Willow (1997), Save the Children (1997, 1999), Boyden and Ennew (1997), Cockburn et al (1997), Howarth (1997), Office of the Children's Rights Commissioner for London (2001, 2002a, b).
9. Ekstedt and Nomura (2002), Swift (1997); Liebel (2004).
10. Karkara and O'Kane (2002).
11. Kellett et al (2004).
12. van Beers (2002).
13. Davis and Hogan (2003), McNeish (1999).
14. Morrow (2001).
15. See Melville and Urquhart (2002).

Section 5: Money matters – contracts, funding projects and paying participants

Sections 1-4 reviewed choices mainly made during the early project design stages before it is possible to apply for funds, although the potential budget is likely to influence the project design very much. These early choices are about the aims, questions and methods of the project, although choice-making often continues into later stages. This section questions the sources of research funds, problems with budgets and timing, and how contracts can protect ethical standards. It ends with questions about paying children and young people for their contributions to consultation or research projects.

5.1 Planning and budgeting

Much ethics guidance sets high standards, but says little about how the complicated and often messy day-to-day conduct of research can fit these standards. One question is whether some sources of funds for projects may be unethical, such as companies whose products harm children.

Management and budgeting involve the efficient and also ethical treatment of the whole project team with care and respect: enabling them to respect the participants, to develop their own ideas, analyse data in depth, and report the research widely. If project teams are too hierarchical, it can be harder for junior researchers, who usually work closest to the young participants, to report any problems they may have, and to get team leaders to attend to these problems.

Contracts with funders for research projects, consultancies and evaluations need to allow for:

- reasonable costing and timing, including funds to allow for inclusive methods, such as the extra time and resources that may be needed for children who speak little or no English, and for children with learning difficulties (Braille, signing or IT communication, taxi and escort fares)[1]

- regular discussion times among the research team
- adequate secretarial, technical and library support and project accommodation
- a pilot or flexible initial period to learn from the research participants' responses and then possibly to improve the project design
- time for collecting and analysing the evidence
- time to report back to the children and young people
- time to write reports for all who have helped with the project, and for wide dissemination to increase the chance that useful findings might be implemented or might affect policies and attitudes.
- a freedom to publish clause (see below).

The new research governance standards in England[2] are promoting generally higher agreed standards in contracts, including the use of a sponsor to oversee the progress of each project. Contracts could include clauses on:

- the researchers' priorities and values
- ethical questions raised by the research and the means of addressing these
- equal opportunities policy, and how cultural, religious, gender, age, disability or other differences among research participants are respected
- a disclaimer for funders in reports, saying that sponsorship does not necessarily mean support for the conclusions
- researchers' intentions to report research problems and actual methods honestly and to be cautious about how reliable and generalisable or transferable the data are
- avoiding fabrication and misrepresentation of data
- reporting in sufficient detail to enable other researchers to understand and learn from the project
- a freedom to publish clause.

The National Children's Bureau Guidelines[3] advise a freedom to publish clause that includes ways to protect the integrity of projects and to respect researchers and sponsors. The guidelines state that:

> Where we approach to undertake a study of a confidential or
> particularly sensitive area [plans for research reports] would need
> to be agreed between the Bureau and the funding agency at the
> outset. All reports will be shown to participating organisations and
> the funding agency in draft form and any comments will be
> carefully considered. [The Bureau] retains the responsibility for
> what is finally written [and] copyright, except where agreed
> otherwise. Evaluative research in particular, by its very nature, will
> often raise questions concerning certain existing policies or
> practices. This will always be presented constructively but
> participating agencies must be prepared for this possibility.

Researchers may produce important but disturbing findings that their own employers do not wish to publish for fear of alienating patrons or funders. Contracts guard against this when they mention researchers' (not only their agencies' or employers') rights to publish. However, another barrier to this freedom is having to satisfy editors, and in academic journals the peer reviewers, before publishing reports in the press.

Many unexpected problems may arise during projects. Foresight, well-thought-out contracts and attention to ethical questions can all partly help to prevent or reduce these problems.

5.2 Paying young researchers and participants

Payments may be made for these reasons:
- to reimburse expenses, including escorts' fares
- to compensate for time, inconvenience and possible discomfort
- to show a token appreciation for participants' help
- to pay for young people's help just as adults are paid.

Some guidelines advise that payments may be made to encourage participants to take part 'as an incentive'. However, such payments would contravene the Nuremberg standards that no persuasion or pressure of any kind should be put on participants. Payments may bribe or even coerce people into taking part. A small payment can mean a great deal to disadvantaged people including many children. They may then feel they have to divulge more than they would choose to, or say more strongly what they think researchers want to hear.

Should people be paid at the start and assured that, whatever they say or do, such as leave the project, the payment stands? Or should payment only be given 'as a surprise' afterwards, when there would be no risk of bribing people? Some funders do not allow payments to be made. However, on the importance of respecting and rewarding young people, see box 7.5.

The pros and cons of paying young people are debated in a review of ethics guidelines that usefully separates the four types of payment – reimbursement, compensation, appreciation and incentive. The review concludes with 11 safeguards, given here for readers to debate. The safeguards aim to reduce the chance that parents' and children's decisions, about whether to join a project, will be distorted by promise of a payment.[4]

1. Develop guidelines for all four types of payment.
2. Adopt an explicit policy on advertising payment to children.
3. Require explicit justification for all incentives.
4. Allow for children to be paid less than adults in identical studies.
5. Ensure payment to subjects who withdraw.
6. Consider carefully any cases where there is concern that people are consenting because of payment and not because they wish to take part.
7. Develop a general policy on describing payments in consent and assent forms.
8. Make direct payments to the proper party.
9. Avoid lump sum payments.
10. Consider deferred payments.
11. Consider non-cash payments.

Children In Scotland[5] gives another example of guidance on payment.

> '4.1 Children in Scotland will refund all reasonable travel and subsistence expenses incurred by informants in the course of participating in the research, on production of receipts.

4.2 Children in Scotland may also pay research contacts
[participants] in addition to expenses as inducement to
participate, as recompense for time, or as appreciation of the
contribution. It may be made in the form of cash, vouchers, or in
the form of a donation or gift to a group, school or other
organisation. In survey research a prize draw may be used as an
inducement to return the form.'

Readers may wish to discuss the mention of inducement and also the
prize draw. Although almost everyone supports lotteries, some people
do not. Does the use of a prize draw therefore complicate the aim that
the research be inclusive?

There seems to be no consensus at all about [paying young
participants], even among young people involved in consultations
or research. Some of them in group discussions about being
involved in research and consultation thought that taking part in
projects should be voluntary, without incentives. Others said that
knowing in advance that they would be paid would encourage
them to take part[6]

One safeguard is when researchers alone do not have to make all the
ethics decisions, but can share them with an ethics review committee,
as considered in section 6.

[1] Porter and Lewis (2001), Davis et al (2000).
[2] DoH (2001).
[3] NCB (1993, slightly less clear in revised 2003 version).
[4] Wendler et al (2002).
[5] Children in Scotland (2002).
[6] MacDougall (2003a).

Section 6: Reviewing aims and methods: ethics guidance and committees

This section is about making the final revisions to research plans, perhaps after pilots or in the light of comments from colleagues and other reviewers. Whereas medical research is informed by research ethics committee (REC) reviews, and detailed guidelines, so far there is less routine formal review for social research. Section 6.2 looks at whether review committees and guidance are useful, and how they might be more useful. As we noted earlier, one aim of this report is to promote discussion among social researchers about the value of collective reviews and guidance.

6.1 Review and revision of research aims and methods

It is now much more generally accepted that children and young people have a great deal of knowledge which can be very useful at all stages of a project, not just during the data collecting phases.[1] Research that is seriously planned with 'insider' children, young people and adults is perhaps more likely to involve relevant questions and ethical methods.

Consultation with users and other reviewers ranges from informal contacts, to committee reviews, to conducting formal pilots. We suggest that there should always be a stage in any research or consultation process when a group reviews the planned project to see if it is ethical and ask:

- are the basic assumptions about children underlying the research positive?
- is there scope for taking real account of children's and adults' comments, and their complaints if these arise?
- who are the researchers accountable to when they justify their work?

Children can advise on a wide range of methods, as recommended in box 6.1.

Box 6.1 Involving children in designing research to promote good science and ethics

A systematic overview of research reports about barriers to, and facilitators of, children's physical activity started with 8,231 titles and abstracts. The reviewers showed that only 69 reported programmes which aimed to increase children's physical activities, had been properly evaluated. And only five evaluations actually showed whether the programmes worked or not – a great waste of resources and opportunities. The review team also concluded that children's own views are rarely heard so that basic data are missing.[2] The team recommended that the views of children aged 4 to 10 years, 'should be the starting point for any future development of efforts to promote physical activity'. 'Where possible children should be asked directly for their views on what could or should be done to promote their...activity.' 'Children, parents and other stakeholders should be involved in planning the evaluation of interventions to physical activity...in determining relevant and appropriate data collection methods, tools and topics, and in determining outcomes to be measured'. The team counted parents' replies on behalf of their children as parents' views (and not necessarily as children's), and said that studies 'need to engage children in a way that honours them as research participants [and] in a dialogue that is meaningful to them'.[3]

6.2 Does social research need research ethics committees (RECs)?

There are networks of medical RECs but so far few social ones. Would these help to raise standards of social research? For discussion, here are arguments for and against RECs, mainly based on the record of medical RECs but which could be considered for social RECs.

How are RECs useful?

■ RECs can help to prevent poor research, safeguard research participants, and be a protective barrier between potential participants and researchers.

■ RECs help to raise awareness and serious concern about ethical standards of research.

■ One effect is that many researchers now consider ethical aspects to be a basic part of research planning and processes, not just an afterthought.

■ By involving laypeople, service users, and people from different disciplines – such as law, philosophy, religion, social science – among their members, medical RECs encourage researchers to be challenged, to take account of differing views and values, and to be accountable to them.

■ Some RECs show that a single committee can cover projects involving a great range of disciplines/professions, methods, theories and topics.

■ RECs help to raise standards of clear information for research participants by vetting research information sheets.

■ RECs can check that the research suits their local area, stop certain groups being over-researched, and see if leaflets in other languages and link-workers should be in the research plans.

■ Review by several RECs (for multi-centre projects) can be a safeguard. Errors and harms overlooked by some RECs are noticed by others.

■ Some disagreement among RECs about questions of ethics and values is inevitable, and can increase ethical awareness through practical debate about actual protocols.

How are RECs not useful?

■ RECs may waste research time and money, especially when multi-centre research has to be submitted to many committees.

■ They can delay projects for months and seriously disrupt research contracts and staffing. (Medical LRECs must now complete review within a maximum of 60 days, many take less time.)

■ There are seldom formally allocated funds for the sometimes high costs of applying to RECs.

- RECs are under-funded and rely on many hours of unpaid work. They can be inefficient. Some lack the experts needed for proper review. (However, medical LRECs have large incomes from drug companies' applications, which subsidise other applications.)
- RECs cannot completely guarantee that ethical research is supported and poor research prevented.
- Some RECs nit-pick over small points and disagree with other committees' decisions about protocols, which suggests that REC review is inefficient and unscientific.
- Social researchers complain that some medical RECs do not understand all main social research approaches and methods.
- RECs can be dominated by a few members who are determined to accept or reject certain protocols.
- There is a danger that researchers may pass on ethical responsibility to RECs, and conduct research which they privately believe is useless or harmful, arguing in public that 'it must be all right it's been approved'.

Box 6.1 Pros and cons of ethics committee review: a personal view
By Dr Cathy Street, YoungMinds

Applying for multi-centre REC review was a useful if very lengthy process. Following the review, we found it essential to give spoken and written reminders regularly to interviewees about their rights to consent, opt out, and change their mind, and that this would not in any way affect their care.

Advantages of applying to the REC

We had to think through how to present clear and concise project information for different audiences, besides the ins and outs of consent before we started. Clinicians/service providers seem more willing to help with a study that has been approved, and it helps to clarify roles.

Drawbacks

The very lengthy form and other papers are overly clinical, designed for drug trials rather than social research. We made long telephone calls to gain advice on completing the forms.

RECs can promote discussion and awareness

Ethics reviews attempt to balance rigorous science with humane respect and compassion, and the interests of present research participants with those of people who might benefit in future. This is partly why RECs sometimes disagree, depending on their memberships. There is not necessarily a correct balance of conflicting values. Working towards reasonable solutions helps to evolve higher ethical standards and reach some consensus.

There are some social RECs, but much social research does not go through any ethics review, creating a double standard. To be effective, widely established and respected, social RECs need to address the following questions, some of which are still unresolved among medical RECs.

- How can the purpose and remit of the REC be agreed or at least respected by all the researchers who apply to them?
- How can reasonable ethical standards and assessment criteria for all the varied disciplines and research methods be agreed?
- How can conflict and rivalry between members be prevented from skewing REC decisions?
- How can social RECs gain credibility, so that they can complement rather than replicate medical REC review for social health research?

Social research communities may decide that these problems are irresolvable and that informal review by an individual or a small group, or no review at all, is preferable. However, this means that social research is conducted amid unresolved problems about ethics, with little or no formal protection for research participants, or for the reputation of social research and of research institutions. Individual or informal small group review may repeat the faults of the least efficient RECs, with the added problems that they can be more arbitrary and secretive.

There is currently no respected social research forum, covering the range of agencies, disciplines and methods, to debate ethical problems, and potentially to aid progress towards resolving problems and promoting higher standards. Medical RECs have a central body: COREC. As already mentioned, social researchers who are concerned about ethics in their work may be isolated and have no collective political voice. Section 11 reviews urgent questions that social researchers cannot resolve on their own. This is a very fast-changing field, and guidance is continually being reviewed and produced.[4] However, a respected social science research central forum could:

- keep summarising new changes in national and international policies
- bring researchers up to date on any major changes
- explain and justify the practical meaning of these changes and how they affect everyday social research and consultations
- help to agree reasonable standards and answers to ethical dilemmas
- help to protect participants, researchers and the good name of social research
- coordinate and validate training programmes for social researchers and REC members
- liaise with medical and other RECs to support positive co-ordination and to avoid wasteful duplication.

[1] Morrow (2001), Borland et al (2001), Hill (2004).
[2] Brunton et al (2003): 104.
[3] Ibid: 102-4.
[4] For example, DoH (2001), EU RESPECT, ESRC.

Part 2

The data collecting stages

Although similar ethical questions overlap through all the stages of research, evaluation or consultation, certain questions are most pressing during the times of direct contact with participants. These are highlighted in Part 2.

Section 7: Information

Section 7 summarises the main details that people who are asked to take part in research need to know in order to be able to give informed consent. It is vital to inform people of all ages clearly.

7.1 Research information leaflets

The details of the research project can be set out in simple leaflets (see Appendix 2). These are also a useful basis for talking about the project and answering further questions with each person. One way to avoid either under- or over-informing (boring) people is to put a core of basic information in the leaflet, with suggestions for further topics to discuss. This can combine what the reasonable researcher would tell, what a prudent person would ask, and what each individual wants to know.[1] Ethics committees often require such leaflets to be shown to them, as the only means of checking that potential participants receive at least basic information. When writing leaflets researchers should talk with the people they are aimed at. What questions do they want raised? What terms do they use?

The leaflets can be given to everyone affected by the research as a short handy guide: to children and young people, parents and carers, other adults such as staff in the school or wherever the research takes place, and to general enquirers. If the same leaflet is clear enough for young children or people with learning difficulties, it can be used for everyone. Such leaflets could also be used by many adults working with or caring for children when they are doing projects, evaluations or routine assessments or case studies, or by journalists making a documentary, or psychologists doing statements with children who have special needs. Many of these children and their parents do not know what a statement is for.[2] Using simple leaflets could help to overcome ignorance, resistance and even fear, and encourage more efficient and respectful working relationships between adults and children and young people.

The leaflets can explain who you are, what you are doing, why and how. This helps children to be prepared and to feel more in control over what is happening. Yet it is important not to assume that people read or remember the leaflets. Researchers often need to talk through the leaflets with children and leave plenty of pauses for questions. Leaflets are an extra resource; they cannot replace discussion. Leaflets often start with what the researcher wants to explain about their research. It is better to put yourself in the children's position and begin by explaining what they might most want to know.

Leaflets and discussions with children who might join the project can include the details in box 7.1. Some of these points have been covered at the start of this report, but here they are included as items to explain to participants. (For a complete list see also box 2.1 on risk/benefit, section 3.3 on privacy and section 8.3 on consent and refusal rights.)

Box 7.1 Title, topics and purpose

Title
Apart from a formal title, does the project have a simple user-friendly, working title? *'A survey commissioned by the local authority social services department of out-of-school provision for children aged 4 to 11 years'* hardly sounds inviting. Children stress that they like the clubs to be as different from school as possible, and this can include renaming their centre from 'out-of-school' to 'The Palace'[3] or 'The A-space'.[4] 'The Palace Project' is likely to attract more interest, and to help young people to feel more involved.

Topics
- What are the main topics areas?
  What are the main questions? Some examples of how to explain topic areas might be:
  Many young people aged under 16 become homeless.
  We hope to learn from them what kinds of help they need.

Each year, many young people are excluded from their school. Why does this happen? We are asking young people, parents and teachers for their views.
Some people in this school have problems with maths. We want to try out a new maths course.

Purpose and aims
- What is the point of asking the questions?
- What do the researchers hope to achieve? – to add to knowledge, to inform policy?
- Is the project worthwhile?
- How are the findings likely to benefit children? (For example?)
- What new questions does this research ask which no other research has yet answered?

Box 7.2 What will happen to people during the research?

Timing
- How long will the project take?
- For how much time will each person be involved?
- How many sessions will there be and where?
- How often and how long will or might these be?

Methods
- What methods will be used? (For example: a tape-recorded interview, a survey, a maths programme, counselling sessions, observations, focus groups, questionnaires, a randomised trial.)
- What kinds of questions might be asked?
  – open or closed or both?
  – about experiences or views?
  – about public or personal matters?

- Do research methods need to be explained and justified? For example:
  - are relevant research terms, such as 'randomised' or 'control group' explained?
  - what is an interview or group discussion expected to achieve?
  - why is the chosen method the preferred one?

Box 7.3 Use of data

- How certain is it that each person's data will be used?
- In qualitative reports, for example, might some people be reported only very briefly or not at all?
- Will people be sent a transcript of their interview if they wish, for them to check and keep?
- Will their photographs or drawings be returned to them?
- When reports are being written, will people be asked to comment, especially if they might be identified or might disagree with the researchers' conclusions?

Box 7.4 Further information

Naming contacts

The leaflet should include the names of:

- the researcher with phone number/email
- the research base with full address
- the sponsors
- the REC and the approved project number, if relevant.

Risks, harms, and indemnity

- RECs require leaflets:
- to state that research cannot offer direct benefits
- to explain any risks or harms

- to give details about researchers' indemnity – if there is serious harm who will pay any costs and compensation? This relates to medical rather than social research.

7.2 Leaflet layout

Clearly written and laid out information can help everyone concerned:
- to discuss the research more fully and clearly
- to decide what questions to ask the researchers
- to understand and remember researchers' spoken information
- to know about the hoped-for benefits of the research and any risks or costs.

Leaflets can help to increase informed public support for efficient research. They help funders and others who assess projects, such as ethics committee members:
- to find out quickly and clearly the essential points about the research
- to assess the value of the project, and the researchers' attitudes towards the participants. The tone and style of the leaflet – how child/young person-friendly it seems – often tell a great deal about this.

The leaflet needs to be written in terms that children can read, or can understand when someone reads it to them. For some projects, a coloured sheet of A4 is folded to make a four-page A5 leaflet. Narrow columns are much easier to read, as newspapers show. A project logo might be added, and perhaps drawings, flow charts, spidergrams, speech bubbles or other useful and cheerful diagrams. Large dark print on white or pale matt – not glossy – paper helps people with poor eyesight, as well as slow readers. Subheadings or a question and answer format also help them, with the messages broken up into short sections. A sheet with fuller details could be tucked inside the leaflet for complicated projects.

Clear leaflets show that researchers are willing to think and write in terms young people prefer, and they allow for people who read little English. Plain language risks being crude, simplistic, patronising and irritating, but it can be worse to use confusing and intimidating language. Clear leaflets use:[5]

- short lines, words, sentences and paragraphs
- one main idea per sentence
- requests rather than commands
- the active voice (we will meet you …) rather than the passive voice (appointments will be booked)
- a personal approach (we, you, your sister) rather than an impersonal one (they, those, he or she)
- specific details rather than vague ones.

The leaflets avoid repetition, negative remarks and 'do nots', alienating labels, jargon and acronyms unless they are explained. Some researchers use Makaton or other sign language to write leaflets for people with learning difficulties[6]. Braille and taped information can be used for blind people, large print for those with partial vision.

7.3 Leaflets in other languages

Translations need to be checked by two or three readers to see that they are clear and accurate, and for their tone and style. Ask one person to translate the text and another to translate it back. Leaflets in other languages should be used with a link worker or interpreter, not alone. Participants can then share their views with the researchers. Interpreters may block, rather than aid, discussion, unless they are well chosen: age, gender, empathy, respect for clients, skill in listening and some knowledge of the research can be vital. Research with people who speak little or no English should include funds for these services. There may be a local multicultural education advisory service that can help. But there is still a problem about which dialect to use, and whether people read as well as speak the language. Other community groups may help. A large project involved interpreters for 27 languages. In the follow up study, the researchers trained the interpreters to conduct the interviews themselves and to be full members of the research team.[7]

7.4 Two-way information exchanged throughout the project

Ethics guidance tends to see information-giving as one-way: researchers inform potential participants. The process is more useful if it is two-way, when researchers listen to participants, sort out misunderstandings, and think with them about how the research could be improved. Data collecting mainly involves children and young people informing the researchers. Towards the end of the project, researchers can report back to them (boxes 7.5, 7.6, 7.7), as part of carefully planned and respectful exchanges throughout the project.

Box 7.5 Respect throughout the project
By Adrienne Katz, Executive Director, Young Voice
We aim to give young people value-status and power equal to adults within each project in a co-operative venture. We consult them even before questionnaires or projects are designed, shaping these in response to the problems as they see them. They are the drivers throughout, alongside specialist agencies, professionals and policy makers.

Of course we will go anywhere to interview a young person, whenever and wherever they choose, providing it is safe and reasonable for them and our researcher. We always provide them with refreshments and pay their travel costs. To protect privacy in our project with parents who are young offenders and prisoners, we try to send a different researcher to talk to each member in the same family/relationship, such as a young man, his girl friend and his mother. The researchers then do not have inside knowledge before meeting interviewees. We use pseudonyms and other disguises in our reports so that people cannot publicise their own relationships and be damaged inadvertently by us.

We treat interviewees as 'consultants' within a project, to avoid implying that we are helping them because they are somehow failing or inadequate. We protect their identities from the media, and structure confidentiality so that even if schools or police ask us, for example, who has admitted to using illegal drugs, we cannot provide the information because we do not have it. We keep names and personal details separate from all the other data. (We have used a borough's ballot boxes to prevent teachers reading people's replies.)

Young people are our constituents and we know we represent their views when publicising our findings and messages. We encourage them to tell us what they think of this at all times via feedback on the website. When possible, representatives of the group present research findings to the media or at seminars, unless this breaches confidentiality. We always struggle to improve these principles and will not work with partners who won't observe them.

For more information on showing respect in a project, see also section 9 and box 9.1.

Reporting back and saying goodbye
Boxes 7.6-7.7 describe ways of validating findings with young people, reporting back to them and drawing what may have been quite close relationships to an end.

Box 7.6 Children and smoking: participant validations
By Beth Milton, PhD student
Towards the end of my longitudinal smoking study (see box 8.5), I presented an age-appropriate summary of my findings to focus groups of the 11 year old participants so that they could discuss and validate the findings. I found this worked extremely well. I was very impressed by their thoughtful discussions and reflections on whether the findings were a valid interpretation of

the data. Several important themes from these discussions were added to, and greatly enriched, my analysis. I would really encourage other researchers to use participant validation.

Box 7.7 Validations to inform the final report

In a project on children's experiences of their urban environments, the researcher and each class discussed a leaflet giving a preliminary analysis. Children were asked if they felt their views were represented fairly and accurately. Sometimes they spoke of strong views they had discussed in groups which were not in the leaflet (in one case, difficult relationships between pupils and teachers). This informed the final written report. These children also wanted to know what would happen to the research.[8]

Researchers of children's perspectives on out-of-school care reported to the children early in the analysis stage[9]. They checked with several of the clubs whether the children agreed with the researchers' inferences about the children's experiences. Unfortunately, the children who originally took part in the research were not always still there, but this process was useful in confirming or challenging adult-defined inferences.

Box 7.8 Closing the relationship

During a project on children's understandings of 'family', the researcher presented a very preliminary general data analysis to each group of children at the end of term, before they dispersed in July. It would be hard to trace them later to provide a fuller report. The children's responses varied. Twice they gave a round of applause, and a hail of requests to see the report. Copies of the report were duly sent to the schools, 18 months later. One group of 8 year old children listened and asked a few questions about words they did not understand. Some 10 year olds astutely asked questions, such as: 'Why did you choose us to work with?' and 'Who will read the report?' They were keen to know when the researcher would visit them again. This raises the difficult (and rarely discussed) issue of how to close what may have become a close working relationship.[10]

7.9 Owning the information

Do children hold copyright, such as for their writing, drawing or photographs? The law seems to be unclear, as minors cannot own property (it must be held in trust for them) and the same appears to apply to copyright. However, respect for children surely involves acknowledging their authorship and their contributions to research and other projects.

In one project, children took about six photographs of places that were important to them (they were asked not to include people in their photographs). They could use the rest of the film for whatever they wanted. The researcher had the cameras processed, and the unopened packets of photos were returned to the photographers. They then sorted out the photos for the research, and using self-adhesive notes, wrote captions on the back of each photo describing why they had taken them. They kept the negatives, and all their other photographs.[11]

Young refugees and asylum seekers took photographs of aspects of the school that helped them most to feel integrated, welcome members of their new community. They matched these to cards printed with articles from the UNCRC, and made photograph albums about their rights at school. The researcher thanked the groups and presented the albums back to them at a school assembly, a way of celebrating their contributions to the research on children's rights and of informing the whole school about the project.[12]

More reporting back

Another way to thank groups of children, such as school classes, is to send large wall charts to display in classrooms or corridors. These can show findings in pie and bar charts, with short notes about the key findings from the school, and alongside them the overall results from all the schools or other groups in the project.[13]

A main purpose for sharing information early on is to ensure that people are able to give valid informed consent or refusal, the topic of the next section.

[1]   Kennedy (1988): 191-3.
[2]   Galloway et al (1994).
[3]   Smith and Barker (2002).
[4]   Mayall and Hood (2001).
[5]   Vernon (1980).
[6]   Cambridge (1993).
[7]   Oakley et al (2003).
[8]   Morrow (2001).
[9]   Smith and Barker (1999): 8.
[10] Morrow (1998).
[11] Morrow (2001), see also Smith and Barker (1999).
[12] Clarke-Jones (2002).
[13] Alderson (2000b).

Section 8: Consent

This section reviews the meanings of 'consent', the legal bases for respecting competent children's consent, and the consent of people with parental responsibility. We discuss methods of assessing children's competence, the levels of their involvement in decision-making, and methods and reasons for requesting and respecting children's consent.

Several problems about consent cannot be resolved by individual researchers alone. These include:

- Can and should researchers sometimes ask only for children's and not also for parents' consent?
- How can children's competence be assessed in ways that convince critics that children's competence and consent are genuine?
- Should there be different standards for consent to medical versus social research, or to academic research versus consultations and evaluations, or for projects conducted by young people, by students or by adults?

These questions are also considered in section 11.

Most writing about consent involves consent to medical treatment and research. We suggest that the same values of respect, trust, clear information and good communication apply to consent in any kind of project. Ethical projects take participants' consent, their informed and freely given 'yes' or 'no', very seriously. In group discussions about research, some young people clearly understood the point of the consent process: 'We need to be able to say "no"'.[1]

One reason to support a common standard of consent is that there is no single measure of the level of risk and complexity of research. To some children, a small project that aims to keep an adventure playground open may be as important, or sensitive, or worrying, as a trial to test a medicine could be. Some small projects can be just as invasive or disrespectful as some large ones.

Respect for consent has been a theme throughout sections 1-7. The careful planning of projects, and the ways of informing and communicating with children and young people all lead up to the question about whether they will take part. This is the time for them to decide, and for researchers to stand back, wait and listen.

8.1 The meaning of consent

Consent has a tragic history[2] (see boxes 1.4-1.5), which helps to explain the following meanings of consent.

- Consent is the central act in ethics. Valid consent is properly informed (Helsinki) and also freely given – without pressures such as coercion, threats or persuasion.[3]
- Respect for consent or refusal helps to prevent harm and abuse, such as people feeling deceived, exploited, shamed, or otherwise wronged by researchers.
- Researchers and participants may define 'harm' very differently. The consent process is the time to clarify any differences. Researchers may then gain new insights into risks and perhaps how to reduce them.
- Potential participants then decide if it is worth taking part in a project despite any risks and costs.
- This process may sound rather extreme for a decision to take part in a small project, but respect for consent sets standards of respect for the whole relationship between the researchers and participants.
- Consent has an impact on all other rights. It is about selecting options and personal preferences, negotiating, accepting or rejecting them. Beyond choosing, consent involves deciding and becoming committed to the decision.
- Much research about consent assesses how people recall and recount the information they were given[4], so it is really about information rather than consent. Consent is the invisible act of evaluating information and making a decision, and the visible act of signifying the decision. Consent may be implied, such as by taking part in an interview or survey. Consultations and social research depend on participants' active co-operation, such as by answering questions, and this could be taken as implied consent.

People may, however, be afraid, or too embarrassed, to say no unless they are given a respectful chance to refuse, withdraw, or agree to take part in some or all parts of the research.

■ In any research, there should be a time for people to be able to ask further questions, to decide, and to say yes or no. Consent may be spoken, or written on a consent form. Participants should have a copy of the consent form and the information leaflet to keep. There could be a space on the form for both parent and child to sign, though some children prefer to give oral, but not written, consent.[5]

■ Consent may be 'one-off' to a single event. For longer projects, such as repeated observations, longitudinal or action research, or trials (including medical trials), or even during an interview or questionnaire, people have the right to change their mind, to withdraw, or to answer some questions but not others. This right should be made clear to them.

Assent Guidance often mentions children's 'assent'. We have not used this term for three reasons. First, assent refers to agreement by minors who have no legal right to consent. However, English law is unusual in that the *Gillick* ruling (discussed below in section 8.3) does not specifically exclude any child as too young to be *Gillick* competent. Children, therefore, who can make informed, 'wise' and *Gillick*-competent decisions are giving consent/refusal rather than assent. Secondly, assent refers to agreement by children who understand some but not all the main issues required for consent. We question whether a partly informed decision can count as a decision at all, or should have what could be a spurious quasi-legal status such as assent. Thirdly, assent can mean 'at least not refusing'. But that can be very different from actually assenting, such as when children are too afraid, or confused, or ignored, to refuse. Again the term assent may be misused to cover over children's refusal.

8.2 Consent and the law

There are no statute laws about research on human beings in the UK, unlike research on animals. The law therefore relies heavily on people to protect themselves by their personal (or parental) consent or refusal.

No law compels social researchers to observe ethics guidelines on consent. Instead, there are other pressures on many researchers to do so, from their funders, their employers, from their professional associations, and from organisations that grant access to participants[6]. If by any chance social researchers were sued, the courts would want to know that reasonable ethical standards had been met. So the ethics guidelines that set out these standards have quasi-legal status. If there is doubt that consent to the research is valid, a signed consent form would be necessary, but not sufficient, evidence. Researchers would also have to show that they gave clear, full information and respected the person's freely made decision.

Informed consent is specific, not a blanket general consent[7] such as 'to anything else the research might involve'. Researchers should explain everything that they ask people to consent to. If the research plans are uncertain at first, researchers should say so. If the plans change, for example if new topics and questions are added, these should be explained and consent to the new plans should be requested. Medical LRECs require researchers to apply for approval of such changes.

8.3 Consent by and for children and young people

The points in 8.2 apply to children and young people, and to parents when they decide for or with their children. There are some differences between consent for and by children and adults.

- Adults have greater freedom to take risks for themselves. Choices made by and for children must be in their best interests[8] or at least not against their interests.[9]
- In English law, minors over the age of 16 can give legally valid consent[10] such as to medical treatment. Competent minors aged

under 16 years can also give valid consent. Competence is defined as having 'sufficient understanding and intelligence to understand what is proposed' and 'sufficient discretion to enable [a child] to make a wise choice in his or her own interests'.[11] Since 1985, the 'retreat from *Gillick*' has undermined respect for competent children. Yet the child's consent to medical treatment can override the parents' refusal.[12]

■ Several experts have advised that the *Gillick* case applies to many other areas of law beyond medical care – and have criticised the undermining of the *Gillick* ruling.[13]

■ When children are competent, 'As a matter of law the parental right to determine whether or not their minor child below the age of 16 will have medical treatment terminates'.[14] Judges see parents as having responsibilities rather than rights, and these are 'dwindling rights' as the child matures.[15]

■ One statute law that respects children's decision-making states that when children are capable of consenting to an application to see their health records, parents may apply only with the consent of the child.[16]

■ The only people who can give legally valid consent are the competent child and people with parental responsibility – parents, and for looked after children the local authority or the High Court.[17] Teachers are *in loco parentis* but do not have parental responsibility. They can grant researchers access to children, but cannot consent to the research.

■ If doctors were sued by parents or other authorities for respecting a child's consent, they can defend themselves legally by claiming that in their clinical judgement the child is competent.[18]

■ Most of the above points refer to treatment but not to research. English medical research guidelines (not the law) advise researchers to ask for parents consent for minors aged under 18 years,[19] but they also emphasise that the young child's refusal to take part in research must be respected.[20]

So there now seems to be a double standard. With medical treatment, the child's consent can override parents' refusal, and the parents' consent can override the child's refusal.[21] But with medical research, the guidance emphasises respect for the refusal even of very young children, which can override the parents' consent.[22]

A theme throughout this report is the balance between concern to prevent and reduce harms in research, and concern about the risks and harms of silencing and excluding children from research about their views, experiences and participation. We suggest that at present, systems do not ensure either adequate protection from harmful or useless research, or adequate participation by children in research that could promote their interests. New attention to children's consent and refusal might help to raise standards, as we review in the rest of this section and in section 11.

8.4 Complications in parents' consent

If a case came to court in which parents and children disagreed about research, no one is sure whether the courts would support a child who wanted either to consent or to refuse against the parents' wishes. Yet only a very risky or controversial example would be likely to reach the courts, in which case researchers would be wise to ask parents too. For some social research, the *Gillick* ruling about respecting the consent of competent children could surely apply, but this standard has not been clearly or formally agreed.

Researchers, in schools for example, may find it hard to insist on requesting parents' and young people's consent, when they depend on the goodwill of the school. Teachers may say that it takes too much time, expense or delay to ask parents, or even to ask young people, who might refuse or not reply. As Hart and Lansdown suggest, 'Adults remain the major barrier to effective participation by children'.[23] However, they add that, with parents, this might be because parents are so often bypassed instead of being informed and involved. 'At a minimum, this means that the chance to involve those who have the greatest impact on children's daily lives [and who can speak for and with children] is lost. But it can have the more damaging impact of creating a struggle of values at home, leading to a backlash against children's rights because parents do not understand them. Sometimes, children suffer punishment for their involvement'.[24] It can be harder for parents who feel disrespected to respect their children. Ethical research involves informing and respecting everyone concerned. If parents refuse, this is a chance for researchers to exchange better information with them. Parents may be right to refuse, and ignoring them can remove protections and advocates for children.

Box 8.2 Parental consent: flexible approaches

Will the consent of one parent alone suffice, especially if they live apart? There is no law that both parents must be asked. In a study about separated families, the researchers usually asked the residential parent. They asked both parents when a child was co-parented (living part-time in two households) or saw both parents often. Yet they found that gaining consent from both parents could often be both impossible and unethically intrusive. They decided to work with the family dynamics, trying not to interfere with them or alter them for the sake of the research.

Some parents and children discussed consent to the research with the 'other' parent as a matter of course. Some parents asked the researchers to contact the other parent; the researchers checked that the other parent did not mind being contacted or having their contact details given to the researchers. But some parents did not want the other parent to know about the research at all.

The researchers respected their wishes, having checked the implications, and that the first parent would be responsible for any potential repercussions. The researchers decided that as long as the child wished to take part, and there were no obvious risks, they trusted the first parent they contacted to decide what was best for that family. They knew that children were adept at moving between separated households and different family contexts and rules. They believed that taking an individual flexible approach, as they went along, tailored to real lives and relationships, was the only way to conduct ethical research with these families.[25]

8.5 Defining and assessing competence to consent

Capacity or competence to consent involves:

- having the capacity to make a choice about a particular proposed treatment
- knowing the risks, benefits, alternatives
- understanding that consent is 'voluntary and continuing permission'[26] and that consent 'can be withdrawn at any time'[27]
- each [person] being informed 'fully, frankly, and truthfully'[28] with 'reasonable care and skill'.[29]

Assessing competence

Competence can be assessed in three ways:[30]

- by status – groups such as adults or very young children
- by function – through tests of reasoning or other ability
- by outcome – if the person makes a choice, which the assessor believes will lead to a reasonable outcome, competence is assumed.

The three ways depend on the assessor's personal views, especially outcome. The manner of testing is important. A highly competent child, who is afraid or angry about being assessed could appear to be incompetent by not co-operating.

Function tests usually assess four standards in the person giving consent:

- mental competence, the ability to understand and decide
- being sufficiently informed
- having sufficient understanding of the case to make a reasoned choice
- voluntariness, having the autonomy to make firm personal decisions based on long term values.

The standards tend to link to *factors specific to each child*, such as age, gender, ethnicity, ability, maturity and personal experience. Adults may also consider children's hopes, fears, values, life-plans, temperament and degree of independence and assertiveness and willingness to take risks.

Yet it is equally vital to consider *factors around the child*. Are children usually encouraged to share knowledge and decisions or not? Are they used to being listened to? What is the research setting like, welcoming or intimidating? What research is being discussed, how complex is it? Have the children been told all the main points (listed in box 2.1, section 3.3, boxes 7.1-4 and 8.3)? These look daunting but can be condensed into clear short leaflets (Appendix 2). If children and parents are to be well informed there may be barriers to overcome. These include finding enough time and a quiet space to talk, people who are skilful and confident about sharing information, overcoming language barriers, using simple words, and responding to children's cues and body language.

The function tests will then also involve assessing the concerned adults.
- Are they competently helping the child to understand and decide?
- Are they sufficiently informed and skilled in explaining the information?
- Do they have sufficient understanding to make a reasoned choice and to understand the reasoning of the child's choice?
- Do they respect children who have competence and autonomy?

A hospital chaplain and former head teacher thought that respecting children's decisions involved transferring power from adults to children, and needed courage and maturity in both adults and children. As an adult, 'Am I big enough to say, "Whatever you choose will be valued...I'll do all I can to support you and we'll go forward together"? It's such a big step for the adult to surrender power to the child.'[31] A study about special education also found that some young children's decisions are taken seriously (box 8.3).

Box 8.3 Respecting a child's choices in education
Susan wanted to be the first person in her family to go to university. She insisted on moving from her local reception class, when 4 years old, where she felt 'smothered and mothered', to be a weekly boarder at a special school. She is blind though, like

---

many children at that school, she is exceptionally far-sighted about life and values. During the research interview, when she was aged 10, she recalled how, 'Mum had to drag me screaming down the [school] drive because I didn't want to go home.' Susan visited several secondary schools to look round them. One was too rigid and unfriendly, she thought, others not academic enough. 'It's a really, really difficult decision,' she said. She decided to board at her present school and during the day to attend a nearby public school. 'It would be a struggle but I would get the hang of it,' she decided. Her father wrote a report explaining the decision for the LEA who approved Susan's choice. A year later she was very pleased with her decision, academically and socially. In some ways, only Susan could make a fully informed decision that took account of her experiences, values and plans.[32]

Before adults can begin to respect children's consent, their accounts, and all their other direct contributions to research, adults have to rethink how and why children are often seen as untrustworthy. Important research about children as witnesses in court has shown that they can distinguish reality from fantasy. Pre-school children, and children with learning difficulties can be reliable witnesses and can recall and reconstruct central events accurately, when they are carefully questioned, treated considerately, and have a 'support person' present.[33] 'A child should be presumed to be a competent witness, unless there is good reason to reach a different conclusion'.[34]

It is hard to demonstrate competence, and easier to spot incompetence. For this reason, it is better to start from a presumption that the school age child is competent when talking with children about the research and their views.[35] The term 'participants' gains real meaning when adults and children become partners in all stages of the research, including the stages of consent and checking competence in ways that protect and respect children. This means checking children's ability and also adults' skill to help children to understand as much as possible. In the terms of box 8.4, the aim is to move from view 1 to include view 2 as well.

Box 8.4 Two views of consent

View 1	View 2
legal contract	negotiation
event	process
facts	awareness
static knowledge	growing knowledge
one way	two way exchange of information
testing the child	enabling the child

8.6 Levels of involvement in decision-making

A problem with consent law is that it is all or nothing. It concerns competent people or parental consent, but says nothing about non-competent people's rights. However, the UNCRC, for example, clearly sets out levels (1-3) that respect all children (and see section 3.5). The levels are:
1. to be informed
2. to form and express views
3. to influence a decision
4. to be the main decider about proposed treatment or care.[36]

In English law, *Gillick* goes beyond the UNCRC to the fourth level.[37] Most children and many adults prefer to stop at stage 3 and to share decision making with people close to them. Yet at any age it can be very distressing to feel forced into a decision against your will. Very young children are able to form views and to understand simple explanations[38], and so they may be competent at level 4.

Degrees of respect for children. Ladders show different levels of involving children, from superficial manipulation of the ignorant child and tokenism, through children being assigned to tasks or decisions but not informed. Next is the level of children being consulted and informed, and finally the levels of participatory research when children are willing and able to share and initiate decisions.[39]

8.7 Requesting and respecting consent and refusal

To help children and parents to give informed and unpressured consent or refusal, they should be told about their rights.

- Consent means being able to say yes or no
- People should have time to decide
- There will be no pressure on them while they decide
- They are welcome to ask questions and discuss their views with a researcher
- They may wish to talk to a friend or other person before they decide
- They can refuse or drop out at any time without needing to give a reason

To help people if they want to drop out, researchers can remind them later, ask if they are happy to carry on, and tell them that this will not affect any care or service they are having that is linked to the research. They will still get the best possible care. Information sheets (see section 7) can also make these points in the following ways.

Asking for consent:

Will you help us with our research?

Will you take part in an interview and fill in three questionnaires?

Will you help us to try out the new maths course?

Are you interested in being in a documentary about students who are excluded from school?

Explaining rights:

Do I have to say yes?

No. It is up to you whether you take part in this project. No one should feel forced to agree. You do not have to give a reason for saying 'no', although giving a reason might help the research.

Before you agree, you need to feel sure that the project is worthwhile. If you are not sure what to decide, take time to think. You may want to talk to other people before you decide.

You may also change your mind, and withdraw from the project at any time. Please tell us if you do so, but again you do not have to say why.

When the research is linked to a service (such as teaching or social work) that the child is already receiving:
If you refuse or withdraw we shall still give you the best care/teaching/services that we can.

Some research involves long-term follow-up, historical and longitudinal review, by continuing use of research data. This may be done by the research team or by other researchers. If follow ups might be done later, should researchers ask people to agree at the start of the project, or towards the end of the first project?

Box 8.5 Consent and young people who do not use speech
In one project, some young people who used a mechanical breathing aid did not use speech; not all of them had a technical communication aid. They used other ways to communicate. Some had carers who interpreted their facial expressions and gestures. Some used home-made alphabet boards. Their carers pointed to each letter until the correct one was reached, and gradually each word was spelt out. The young people were able to give informed consent using these methods. Interviews were lengthy and tiring, so they were held over two visits. How could the young people's views be conveyed vividly when they could not give verbatim quotes? A young art student of about the same age listened to the scenarios the young people had described, and drew cartoons about them. One showed how carers may unnecessarily restrict the lives of the young people. They said they felt the cartoons powerfully portrayed their views and experiences.[40]

Box 8.6 Children and smoking: assent and whole-class research
by Beth Milton a PhD student
'My school-based longitudinal study of 250 children's experiences of smoking when aged 9-11 used multiple quantitative and qualitative methods: questionnaires, draw and write with whole classes, focus groups and interviews. How could I ensure that the children could refuse or opt-out during the research? I used three protective layers of permission (head teachers, parents and children's assent). However, assent was a problem in the schools, particularly for whole-class methods. In one class, many children did not want to draw and write, but their teacher insisted that they did the exercise, and gave sweets to everyone to ensure compliance. As a visitor in the classroom I was unable to overrule the teacher, and I also felt compromised by my desire to collect data from each child. In general, I think it is difficult to talk about assent in a whole class, without provision for some children to refuse, perhaps by moving to another room, though this would be hard to achieve in many primary schools. This raises ethical issues, as assent should be genuine with a real opportunity to opt-out, but this often clashes with the usual power relationships between teachers and pupils, especially when teachers are keen to ensure 100 per cent participation.'

8.8 Why respect children's consent?

Respect is a basic ethical principle. Listening to children can help adults to discuss and resolve children's misunderstandings. This can reduce the coercion of resisting or resentful children, and the risk of complaints. Transparent discussion can encourage consent as informed willing commitment by children and young people to a project they understand. Their active co-operation and contributions are then likely to support more efficient and effective research. They are less likely to withdraw from a project. Researchers may gain vital knowledge from children about ways to improve the research.

Some guidance permits covert research.[41] We suggest that this relies on old unethical views and methods that treat research subjects as ignorant objects. Mentioning that their consent should be requested after covert research misunderstands the true meaning of consent as a free choice with the right to refuse. Researchers who respect children's consent and feel accountable to them are more likely to take their views seriously throughout the research. We also suggest that informed partnerships, when researchers have to explain and be accountable for their plans and methods, are more likely to improve the research aims, theories and methods, than covert approaches can do. Research findings and conclusions too may be more accurate when discussed openly with children and young people, such as about their motives even for deviant or criminal activities. In the next example, researchers could have drawn misleading adult-centred conclusions if they had not consulted the children as partners (box 8.7). Although it is a minor issue, it shows the value of explicit over covert research.

Box 8.7 The book corner
Researchers showed children photographs of each main area of their family centre. They asked the children which area they liked best and least. The book corner was the least popular area. The children's replies might be taken as evidence of their immaturity, or a signal to improve the books or the corner. On talking with the children, the researchers found that they disliked the way the corner was used. When the staff were busy, they sent the children to sit there quietly. The children were bored when they had to sit in a large group listening to a story that did not interest everyone. So the staff changed the ways they used the corner and arranged the story groups.[42]

When researchers give clear information to children, this can also help parents to make more informed decisions about whether their child should take part in research. It reduces the risks of parents feeling confused, uncertain and perhaps intimidated into permitting dubious research on children. If necessary, parents are then better able to help and support children during the research.

Researchers who do not respect children's consent or refusal may well hold and perpetuate mistaken and unethical prejudices against children. Realistic research that respects children's social and moral competence challenges prejudices, misleading stereotypes and harmful discrimination. It helps to promote ethical standards of respect and justice.

Ethics guidance tends to emphasise consent during the data collection stages of research, but the later stages when research findings are disseminated and could influence society also have important effects on children, which researchers could address when requesting consent. These are the topics of the next two sections.

1   MacDougall (2003).
2   Faden and Beauchamp (1986).
3   Nuremberg (1947).
4   Hastings Center (1999).
5   Alderson (1993).
6   *Code of Practice Pursuant to Section 118(4) of the Mental Health Act 1983* (1990).
7   Ibid.
8   *Gillick* (1985).
9   Nicholson (1986).
10 Family Law Reform Act (1969).
11 *Gillick (*1985).
12 In re R (1991) 3 WLR 592, in re W (1992) WLR 3 758-82.
13 Lawson (1991), Douglas (1992), Montgomery (1992).
14 *Gillick* (1985).
15 Denning (1970).
16 *Access to Health Records Act* (1990).
17 *Children Act (England and Wales)* (1989).
18 *Age of Legal Capacity Act (Scotland)* (1991).
19 RCP (1990); RCPCH (1992/2000); BMA (2001).
20 RCPCH (1992/2000).
21 In re R (1991), in re W (1992).
22 RCP (1986, 1990, 1990a RCPCH (2000) BMA (2001).
23 Hart and Lansdown (2002).
24 Ibid (2002): 10.
25 Smart et al (2001).
26 *Code of Practice Pursuant to Section 118(4) of the Mental Health Act 1983* (1990).
27 Ibid: 15.12.
28 Ibid: 15.11.
29 Ibid: 15.13.
30 Brazier and Lobjoit (1991).
31 Alderson (1993): 143.
32 Alderson and Goodey (1998): 119-20.
33 King and Yuille (1987), Murray (1988).
34 Scottish Law Commission (1988): 82.
35 Alderson and Montgomery (1996), RCPCH (2000), BMA (2001).

[37] Alderson and Montgomery (1996).
[38] Dunn (1998), Miller (1996).
[39] Hart (1992).
[40] Noyes (1999).
[41] BPS (2000), BSA (2003).
[42] Miller (1998).

Part 3 The reporting and follow up stages

Section 9: Disseminating and implementing the findings

This report follows ethical questions as they arise through the stages of projects.

Sections 1-8 dealt with early planning, and setting standards for every stage of the project. Instead of writing separate sections about the data collection, analysis, and writing up stages, we leave readers to draw on sections 1-8 for questions that arise in these mid-project stages. Justice and respect are key themes while you decide how to select, present and interpret the items in your reports. We now move on to the end-of-project and after-project stages.

Section 9 considers the meaning of dissemination and how it goes beyond writing reports. Research with and by children and young people offers exciting dissemination opportunities. These include exhibitions of children's art and design, photographs and videos, and public presentations of their research through lectures, poems, games and drama, at meetings, and on radio and television. Dissemination involves publicity, maybe meetings and conferences, and perhaps using the mass media to promote public debates about the project.

Dissemination raises important ethical questions. We list some of these, propose possible solutions and review a range of methods. Do people have an ethical duty to try to make their project findings widely known and, if possible, acted on? We also look at methods for critical readers to use before they decide whether to disseminate other people's research findings by applying them through their own work.

9.1 Dissemination: getting to the heart of debate and change

A published project report may reach only very few people. Dissemination – which means sowing seeds – is more widespread and has deeper effects than publication alone. Projects with children often raise emotive, political and ethical debates because, openly or not, they are concerned with inequalities between adults and children and whether these are fair and beneficial. So the seeds, the ideas that are spread around by project findings, are not simply thoughts for people's minds, they also involve deeply-held beliefs and feelings. Projects that aim to sow the seeds of change in policies, services, or beliefs about children and young people have to involve people at a thinking and also a feeling level. This can challenge and upset some of them.[1] At the heart of dissemination of, and debates about, projects for and with children are the tensions (that also arise throughout this report) between promoting children's participation and also protecting them.

9.2 Dissemination and implementation: children, young people and adults working together for change

During many projects, there is little time to write reports, let alone to discuss the findings at conferences and other meetings with people who plan policies and work with children. One way round this problem is to include these activities as a central part of the funded research project, involving children and young people and experienced practical adults from the start. Box 9.1 gives an example from Liverpool that involved disabled young people, the Children's Society and university researchers.

Box 9.1 Disabled children and young people and council policy
The Disability and Diversity group project aims to move the local authority and agencies on, from involving young disabled people only in short consultations and quick fixes towards continuous shared service planning, decisions and delivery. Through forums, newsletters, IT networks, and advocacy, they are together developing agreed standards and a culture that promotes and values young people's participation. Children and young people identify their own agendas and develop their own methods for expressing their views. Deaf children, for example, only chose to join in because a British Sign Language interpreter

---

they knew was involved. The young people advise on services such as integration, advocacy, transition and review processes, on packages of care and responding to complaints. About 40 people aged 9-21 took part in group discussions, conducted by people aged 16-21 years.

The group has raised £150,000 for inclusive creative projects. It has set up an art and drama project, peer education/counselling and disability equality training for staff and pupils in schools, independent advocacy and support across local services and access checks on local buildings and events. They run apprenticeships for disabled young people to become access auditors. There are now more equal power relationships and partnerships between adults and young disabled people. The project shows how active, imaginative and creative they can be.

However, the researchers wonder if the group is representative enough, and if it will last. Partly for lack of time and funds, they found it hard to involve the young people in evaluating and reporting the project (using multi-methods[2]). The researchers also warn of hidden dangers in altering power relations through participatory projects. They stress that the serious work of changing society must be mixed with creativity and fun, to stop 'participatory' projects from oppressing young people.[3]

Box 9.2 Children's views of London
The Office of Children's Rights Commissioner for London (OCRCL) based its work on the UNCRC. Young people were trained about their rights and how to participate politically in important ways, such as being actively involved in Greater London Assembly meetings. These young people then trained others. The OCRCL's large survey conducted by and with young Londoners covered problems of poverty, racism, poor housing, schools, transport and environmental planning, and the lack of

> resources and services for young people, as well as ways for young people and adults to work together to prevent the causes of crime.[4] As a result of their work, the Mayor of London agreed to work with children and young people to develop a city-wide Children's Strategy.[5]

9.3 Problems with dissemination and some potential solutions

Many difficulties can stand in the way of dissemination. Here we list some common problems, with some suggestions of creative solutions.

- Funders or other authorities may stop reports from being published.
  - Include a right-to-publish clause in the project contract or agreement with funders and employers (see section 5).
- People may dismiss reports saying that they are distorted.
  - Ask critical friends to check the project reports and revise the report to answer their criticisms.
- Dissemination can involve months or years of working with policy makers and practitioners, at conferences and other meetings, on how to link research findings and conclusions into their work. Few researchers have the time or funding to do this.
  - Include funds, time, and possibly training, to enable researchers to publish their work for different relevant groups, including short reports for the children and parents[6], for professionals working with them, and for magazines or television programmes they are likely to see.
- Links between the research evidence, the report, and what it means for policy and practice are often unclear. Many researchers prefer to leave practical experts to work out the links but few of these experts have the time or interest to read project reports and to do this connecting work. The reports may remain unused.
  - Researchers and practical experts can learn much from one another when they discuss how to link research to policy and practice. For example, researchers may then be able to write more relevant and practical reports. These discussions can be

valuable extra stages of research projects to recognise and fund. Further projects may be planned. One example is the current rapid change in policies about children's rights and participation, from national government to small local group levels. The changes were promoted by NGOs' practical research projects and publicity about children's rights.

- People may misunderstand and misapply the findings of research or consultation.
  - Researchers' taking part in professional, policy and public debates about their projects helps to increase other people's understanding and use of their findings. The debates may also help researchers to see how to make their reports more convincing and readable.

- The mass media can be very helpful with dissemination, but they may present over-simple, sensational or inaccurate reports.
  - Over-simplification and distortion can be a big problem. You might find an informed journalist who supports children's rights to write about your project. We suggest that problems with the media are too complex for individuals alone to resolve (see 9.4 and section 11).

- Busy people have so much to read that they prefer short clear reports. However, it is often hard to report complex projects in short simple terms.
  - Reports written at different levels and lengths: academic, practical and popular, reach more readers. Writing short reports for research participants helps researchers to analyse and sum up their work clearly. See the Joseph Rowntree Foundation website (www.jrf.org.uk) for examples of *Findings*, very clear four-page project summaries. Page 1 lists about six key points, pages 2-3 explain each point, and page 4 gives details about the methods and outcomes, and the research team. *Findings* are backed up by longer reports, so that readers can choose their reading level depending on their interest. Abstracts at the start of journal articles offer another layered approach. Abstracts are far more widely read and quoted than the full papers, especially those on websites. Their accuracy is therefore very important.

■ The project may not be worth disseminating. It may repeat other work, or be unfinished or unconvincing.

 – The problem of projects that do not produce reports worth publishing shows the importance of careful planning of the project aims, methods and ethics from the start. Reports need to be clear and transparent about the methods and about any limitations of the project. For example, it is important in small projects not to over-generalise from the findings. A study of 50 young carers cannot claim that 'all young carers tend to be depressed' even if all those in the study say that they are sometimes depressed.

■ Editors may refuse to publish the research if it is unethical, such as by being conducted without consent, or if they think a report is poorly written or boring. The findings may be unpopular, or disbelieved, or attacked and dismissed.

 – Research findings that are surprising, counter-intuitive, and genuinely challenge or refute popular views can make vital contributions to knowledge, to theory, evidence, policy and practice. Yet they may be the hardest kind to publish, and may suffer from unfair criticism.

Box 9.3 Multi-level research reports

Dissemination is aided by multi-level reporting. For example, a study of girls' experiences of managing menstruation in school, including their problems in co-educational secondary schools, involved a large sample and combined quantitative and qualitative methods. The project was reported in a policy-related book with a series of recommendations for schools and health education[7], theoretical papers[8], policy recommendations and contributions to a teaching pack. Every girl who took part in the study was sent a copy of a clear four-page article about the project.[9]

9.4 Dissemination and the mass media

The mass media can be very helpful – and sometimes very unhelpful – when publicising projects. Journalists ask for a personal story and want to talk to children and young people who took part in the project. This raises problems about confidentiality (section 3). Young people are often keen to be in the news, but researchers must be wary of serious risks. If children and young people can identify themselves in public reports, or be identified by others:[10]

- they may feel very upset by the way they have been portrayed
- they or their group or school may attract unwanted publicity
- other people may contact them, and exploit, threaten or even harm them
- they may be upset or angry about mass media misreports.

On the other hand, children and young people may enjoy the publicity, feel very pleased about their success, and perhaps achieve the policy changes they aim for with the help of media support. Young Voice finds positive ways to promote these kinds of potential benefits (box 9.4).

Box 9.4 Working positively with the media
by Adrienne Katz, Young Voice www.young-voice.org.uk
We try to work with the media to produce fair and respectful reports. This is a complex and difficult aim. It is impossible to 'control' the media in any way, but the following approaches help.
- Choose your target journalists by following their work over time. Avoid intrusive or sensationalist ones. Meet them about once a year to discuss your current work. Be clear about your way of working, such as not giving them names of young people to order. You could offer them good practice guidelines for the press, such the ones by The Samaritans[9].
- When a journalist asks to talk to young people, and you have someone who wants to do media work, check with them first,

---

then give them the journalist's telephone number (if you approve of that person!). Never give the journalist the young people's numbers. For people under 16, get their parents' permission too. Be clear that they can withdraw and are not doing it just to please your organisation or project.

■ Discuss their rights with the young people. They may be able to insist on seeing the copy before it goes to print. Do they realise that they might be misquoted? Should they keep a note or record of what they say? If the issue is sensitive, offer to go with young people to the interview, though not to sit in on the session.

■ If they have a long journey to meet journalists, we ensure they have a meal and perhaps a good day out with shopping vouchers or a trip to the London Millennium Wheel or other options they choose. Then we can offer support after an interview that might have been upsetting, such as about prison experiences[12] or depression. We often give them a thank you voucher for the time they have given. (We also give vouchers in return for their drawings or photographs they provide.)

■ If a newspaper requests a photo we supply ones that we own all rights to, or we contact the young person who owns it, and negotiate a fee from the paper for them. All young models in our photographs have signed a form that consents to various uses of this image. Parents also sign along with people aged under 16. If there is a broadcasting fee, we try to get it for them.

■ We never hold personal details on file alongside an interview or questionnaire, and so we would never be able to give police or anyone else information relating to an individual's replies to us.

9.5 Critical readers and viewers

The final part of this section reviews how policy makers, people working with children and young people, and journalists interpret and apply research findings. Their responses vitally affect how research is understood and used. Box 9.5 lists methods for critical readers to use when deciding which ideas from reports to accept and apply, and so disseminate through their work.

Box 9.5 Questions for critical readers

- Is the research effective and not a waste of time and resources? For example:
  - Does the research method fit the aims and questions and connect these clearly to the findings and conclusions?
- Are the links clearly argued?
- Do the samples or cases provide enough evidence to support the conclusions?
- What models of childhood and youth do the authors explain or imply that they hold? Respectful, realistic, positive or negative?
- Do the researchers treat the young people as research objects, participants or co-researchers?
- How did the researchers think about and try to resolve any ethical problems?
- What do they say about consent?
- Do they thank the young people who helped with their project in their reports?

Underlying attitudes to children and the three Ps

Children's rights can be divided into the three Ps: Protecting children and young people, Providing for them, or encouraging them to Participate, such as by expressing their own views and contributing to their families and communities. The three Ps partly overlap and are often complementary but carry different emphases. Which of the three Ps do the authors emphasise in the topics, methods and

findings of the research? Authors' views of these three kinds of rights can test how they see and relate to children:
- as victims or problems who need Protection and control
- as dependents in need of services and other Provision
- as Participants who share in defining and solving problems.

[1] Miller (1998).
[2] Davis (1998).
[3] Davis and Hogan (2003a).
[4] OCRCL (2001, 2002a, 2002b).
[5] Mayor of London (2004).
[6] DoH (2001a).
[7] Prendergast (1994).
[8] Prendergast (1995).
[9] Kingsman (1992).
[10] Boyden and Ennew (1997).
[11] Samaritans (2002).
[12] Katz (2002).

Section 10: The impact on children

Most ethics guidance is concerned with the personal cost and benefit to participants during the data collecting stage (section 2). Much less is said about the ethics of the probable impact of the published reports, either on children in the study or on related groups of children and young people. How might they stand to gain or lose? Research can affect very large numbers of children, beyond the individual researcher-child relationship, when influencing public and media opinion and professional policy and practice. For example, do research reports about teenage parents or street children increase respect and practical support for them, or increase prejudice against them? Although researchers cannot wholly control the way their findings are used, they can select the issues they examine, the questions and methods, the ways they interpret their findings, and the terms they use.

This section reviews the social context of research with children and young people, the collective impact research reports can have on them, and the sometimes unintended impacts. We consider what it means to share power with children and young people, and we end by reviewing the use of positive images.

All social research and consultations have political aspects, such as examining how equally knowledge, resources and control are shared. Traditional work on the family that seemed neutral has been shown to be adult-centred, when projects look specifically at the children rather than the single family unit. They find, for example, that children rarely have an equal share of space and resources at home, or in society. Whereas many old people have several rooms to themselves, young children tend to live in homes with less than one room per person.[1] Debates about ethical research involve reviewing how projects show up or cover over such inequalities between adults and children (see earlier sections, especially section 4).

10.1 What collective impact can research have on children?

The impact of research includes both the effects on young research participants during projects and also the longer-term effects on attitudes towards all similar children and young people, and services for them. These effects may be intended or unintended.

One example is medical research charities' use of images in advertising. Charities raising funds for research into cystic fibrosis have often used images of thin, sickly children. But thanks to medical research, most children with CF no longer look thin or sickly and many expect to live into their 40s. These adults are unhappy that public stereotypes stop people from seeing them as employees, mortgage holders and partners. 'I'm tired of people at parties, when they learn I have CF, saying "So why aren't you dead yet?"' commented one young women.[2]

Media reports tend to view children as victims or problems. Few reports show their successes, examine how many problems arise from social attitudes, or show young people's own reasons for their activities. Many researchers feel wary about reporting their work with children in the media in case it is presented unfairly. This question, of whether to keep quiet or to risk being misreported in ways that could harm young people, is one that researchers can hardly resolve individually (though see box 9.4) and it will be considered further in section 11.

Another problem is that reports may have little or no impact. Implementation takes time and is complex. A recent review reported that several imaginative and creative consultations were conducted in Liverpool from 1997 to 2002 (see box 9.1). Children gave competent views about a range of services they receive, and about how the city could be improved. However, 'children and young people have been giving the same key messages to decision makers for several years, and... despite this, there is little evidence of [any] impact on the development of strategic plans in the major service areas of health, education and social services'. The author recommends basic change, a progression from children being consulted to children participating in making decisions within appropriate new structures.[3]

10.2 Reviewing the impact of research on children

Two key questions for ethical review about how research affects children are:
■ What will the planned and possible impact of the research reports be on children and young people, those in the project or in related groups?
■ In some cases, should the research be done at all?

Governments have to report to the UN Committee on the Rights of the Child every five years on their progress in implementing all aspects of the UNCRC. Perhaps a similar overview or audit report could be made regularly on research and consultation with and about children and young people. It could cover:
■ the main areas, disciplines and agencies concerned
■ sources and amount of funding
■ research on matters that affect children but which took account only of adults
■ issues important to children that are not researched
■ methods and values in projects about or with children
■ who gave consent
■ involvement of children and young people in any of the stages of the projects from planning to implementation
■ general trends in the data and conclusions that have positive, neutral or negative emphases
■ links or lack of links with policy and practice
■ mass media reports of projects
■ how the projects promote positive or negative views of childhood and youth.

Even if only a few of the largest social funders and research centres produced such reports, the findings could help future ethics and policy reviews and planning.

When projects do have lasting effects, children may be influenced in three ways.
■ The policies affect children now.

- They may affect children in future when they are adults and see the impact on their own children.
- The effects may last into the far future when today's children are old, long after the researchers have gone.

This entitles children to have an even greater share in helping to plan current research and future policies.[4]

10.3 Positive images

From the mid 1990s, leading NGOs have aimed to use positive pictures, such as active children collecting water instead of helpless starving babies. They have promoted respect for children's dignity through images that avoid stereotypes and sentimental or demeaning pictures of dependency that do harm as well as good. This positive policy can also apply to research in its topics and themes, headings, questions, and the language and tone of its reports.[5]

The National Children's Bureau advocates multi-disciplinary research which attends to 'the whole child'. The Bureau's priorities and principles aim: to 'promote equal opportunities in research'; to seek to 'eradicate prejudice and discrimination against children' of all kinds; to avoid stereotyping; to 'make efforts to ensure that we do not exclude particular groups of people, for instance because there are communication difficulties; and to highlight issues of discrimination and/or injustice in our studies'[6] There are guides to conducting inclusive research with disabled people.[7] These approaches can inform every stage of research from first plans to final publicity.

The final section of this report sums up practical points to suggest future policy for all concerned with social research with children and young people to consider.

[1] Qvortrup et al (1994), Gordon et al (2000), Hood (2002).

[2] Alderson (1998).

[3] Donnelly (2003): 3, Kirby et al (2003).

[4] As the Children's Forum claimed at the UN General Assembly Special Session on Children in May 2002 www.unicefusa.org/ssc/forum.html.

[5] For example see NCH (2001 a, b).

[6] National Children's Bureau, (1993, 2003).

[7] Beresford (1997), Morris (1998), Ward (1997).

Section 11 Conclusion

Since the first version of this report was published in 1995, there has been very welcome growth in:
- research and consultation directly with and by children
- reporting of children's own views and experiences
- the range of methods used with children and by them
- lessons from research by NGOs with children in other continents
- respect for children's rights and participation
- concern about ethics in social research and consultation.

We look forward to perhaps even greater changes over the next nine years.

11.1 Ways forward for individuals and teams

We suggest that the priorities for the future should be to encourage and develop the following trends.
- Growing understanding among researchers about using ethical questions and standards in every aspect of research.
- Willingness to raise ethical research standards through seeing the advantages, rather than through fear about the risks of ignoring the standards.
- Increase in participatory research with children, when the ethics of justice and respect for rights, methods and outcomes, all reinforce one another.
- Public, media and policy attention to research about children's competence, making for more informed, respectful and inclusive communities.
- Concern to check for the impact on children during projects, and to plan new standards based on respect for children.
- Greater concern from policy makers and people working with children and young people to apply the findings of ethical research and consultations.

11.2 Questions that cannot be solved by individuals alone

Most of the goals in section 11.1 can be achieved by individuals and project teams alone. However if certain further questions are to be addressed adequately, they need support from higher authorities. These questions include:

- When can we rely on children's consent and not also need to ask for parents' consent?
- Can we involve children who consent if their parents refuse?
- Are there fairly simple, agreed methods to check if children are competent to consent to join a project?
- Should students doing undergraduate and masters degrees be allowed to do research directly with children and young people, given the lack of time for meeting reasonable ethical standards?
- How can respect for children through the projects' processes, aims and impacts, be taken more seriously by people who plan, fund and vet the projects?
- Can current policies about research and about routine training of students be revised, when these involve covert or distressing methods and negative questionnaires?
- Could funders more routinely support the extra costs of ethical, inclusive projects with children, that prepare and follow up the work with them? And how can funders and researchers promote higher ethical standards in very low-cost short projects?
- Can double standards, of careful REC review for some projects and no review for others, be justified?
- Can researchers and journalists work together more to promote accurate and respectful media reports of research with children and young people – just as journalists now avoid racism and sexism?

11.3 The need for social research ethics authorities

There are several reasons why individuals and project teams alone cannot answer the above questions. The questions do not have simple answers based on logic and evidence. Instead, they involve values, justice, respect, protection, and vested interests. Health researchers now accept that questions of ethics are not decided convincingly either by individuals or by remote elite groups alone, because other groups may challenge them. Researchers cannot, for example, side-step patients' consent simply by saying, 'Trust me I'm a researcher'. To convince critics, they need a general climate of firm support for agreed standards from respected, independent authorities such as RECs.

To be credible, RECs acknowledge the sometimes conflicting interests of participants, researchers and research, and aim to respect the participants' interests first. RECs include members from a range of backgrounds who challenge one another. They debate disagreements and negotiate ethical standards among all stake holders, through compromise and towards consensus. Education and explanation are needed to encourage all concerned to accept and 'own' new standards – in a large-scale version of the consent process, with respect for all participants. There needs to be a continuing political process of revising and raising standards and meeting the challenges of new areas of research. These include collaborations, such as international and interdisciplinary projects; new topics such as genomics or biobanks or the views of the youngest children; new research media such as the internet.

Health care researchers tended to dismiss research ethics 20 years ago, but now they widely regard REC approval as an essential and useful protection. The system can still be very flawed[1] but is generally accepted as better than no system at all. Will social research adopt a similar and better system?

To summarise the points in 11.3 so far, we suggest that:
- stronger social research ethics authorities are needed, to promote higher standards
- the authorities need to be, and to be seen as, reasonably independent and impartial, for example by including a range of stake holders
- they have to work through negotiation and consensus, through explanation and education, so that those concerned gradually come to 'own' and consent to, or at least accept, the agreed standards

- the authorities can be essential ethical mediators in the very unequal relationship between researchers and research subjects
- they help researchers to be accountable and to recognise and aim to meet ethical standards.

Some local social RECs and the relevant national agencies are already working on these activities. We conclude by proposing that their work could be clarified, consolidated and strengthened by a national forum for social research ethics. The forum would:

- cover all the main disciplines and professions in social research
- include representatives from leading funders and commissioners, professional associations, and from government, voluntary, academic and commercial research agencies
- involve research participants as lay members, and preferably have a lay chair
- involve experts on ethical and legal matters
- work out the best ways to learn from and collaborate with health RECs
- have adequate funding
- agree and periodically review and revise national guidance through wide consultation
- promote meetings, training, courses and debates about social research ethics
- promote efficient networks of local RECs
- approve which kinds of social research and consultation, if any, need not go through REC review
- advise on difficult questions that local RECs cannot resolve (see 11.2)
- work with national agencies, such as government and the mass media, on linking research to policy, practice and public debate.

The forum could perhaps consult at national level with service providers about why repeated projects report children's and young people's views but are still ignored.

And finally

Throughout this report we have aimed to balance attention to ways to protect children and young people and prevent and reduce harm, with ways to respect and involve them and to avoid silencing and excluding them. We suggest that present systems do not adequately either protect children from harmful and useless research, or promote their participation and their interests. We suggest that most of our review about children also applies to all other research participants, especially disadvantaged ones. We hope that the Ten Topics (appendix 1) and this whole report will promote local and national debates and action on raising ethical standards in social research and consultation.

[1] Sharav (2003).

Appendix 1 Ten topics in ethical research

Here is a summary of the practical questions raised through the 10 main chapters of this report.

1. The purpose of the research

- What is the research for?
  - to learn more about children's and young people's views, experiences or abilities?
  - to develop or evaluate a service or product?
  - some other positive purpose?
- Whose interests is the research designed to serve?
- If the research findings are meant to benefit certain children, who are they and how might they benefit?
- What questions is the research intended to answer?
- Why are the questions worth investigating?
- Has earlier research answered these questions?
- If so, why are the questions being re-examined?
- How are the chosen methods best suited to the research purpose?

2. Costs and hoped-for benefits

- What contributions are children asked to make to the research? For example, will activities or responses be tested, observed or recorded?
- Might there be risks or costs?
  - time, inconvenience, embarrassment, intrusion of privacy, sense of failure or coercion, fear of admitting anxiety?
- Might there be benefits for children who take part in the research?
  - satisfaction, increased confidence or knowledge, time to talk to an attentive listener?
- Are there risks and costs if the research is not carried out?

- How can the researchers promote possible benefits of their work and prevent or reduce any risks?
- How will they respond to children who wish to refuse or withdraw, or who become distressed?
- Are the research methods being tested with a pilot group?

3 Privacy and confidentiality

- How will the names of children be obtained? Will they be told about the source?
- Will children and parents be able to opt in to the research (such as by returning a card if they wish to volunteer)? Opt out methods (such as asking people to phone to cancel a visit) can be intrusive.
- Is it reasonable to send reminders or can this seem coercive?
- Will research directly with individuals be conducted in a quiet, private place?
- Can parents be present or absent as the child prefers?
- In rare cases, if researchers think that they must report a child's confidences – such as when they think someone is in danger – will they try to discuss this first with the child?
- Do they warn all children that this might happen?
- Will personal names be changed in records and in reports to hide the child's identity?
- What should researchers do if children prefer to be named in reports?
- Will the research records, notes, tapes, films or videos be kept in lockable storage space?
- Who will have access to these records and be able to identify the children?
  – Using post codes instead of names does not protect anonymity.
- When significant extracts from interviews are quoted in reports, should researchers first check the quotations and commentary with the child or parent concerned?
- What should researchers do if respondents want the reports to be altered?
- Before researchers spend time alone with children will their police records be checked?

- Should research records be destroyed when a project is completed, as market and medical researchers are required to do?
- Is it acceptable to re-contact the same children and ask them to take part in another project?

4. Selection, inclusion and exclusion

- Why have the children concerned been selected to take part in the research?
- Do any of them belong to disadvantaged groups?
  - If so, has allowance been made for any extra problems or anxieties they may have?
- Have some children been excluded because, for example, they have speech or learning difficulties?
- Can the exclusion be justified?
- If the research is about children, is it acceptable only to include adult subjects?
- Are the research findings intended to be representative or typical of a certain group of children?
- If so, have the children been sufficiently well selected to support these claims?
- Do the research design and the planned numbers of children allow for refusals and withdrawals?
  - If too many drop out, the research is wasted and unethical.

5. Funding

- Should the research funds be raised only from agencies that avoid activities that can harm children?
- Does the funding allow for time and resources to enable researchers
  - to liaise adequately with the children?
  - to collect, collate and analyse the data efficiently and accurately?
- Are the children's and parent's or carers' expenses repaid?
- Should children be paid or given some reward after helping with research?

6. Review and revision of the research aims and methods

- Have children or their carers helped to plan or comment on the research?
- Has a committee, a small group or an individual reviewed the protocol specifically for its ethical aspects and approach to children?
- Is the design in any way unhelpful or unkind to children?
- Is there scope for taking account of comments and improving the research design?
- Are the researchers accountable to anyone, to justify their work?
- What are the agreed methods of dealing with complaints?

7. Information

- Are the children and adults concerned given details about the purpose and nature of the research, its methods and timing, and the possible benefits, harms and outcomes?
- If the research is about testing two or more services or products are these explained as clearly and fully as possible?
- Are research concepts, such as 'consent', explained clearly?
- Are children given a clearly-written sheet or leaflet to keep, in their first language?
- Does a researcher also explain the project and encourage them to ask questions, working with an interpreter if necessary?
- Does the leaflet give the names and address of the research team?
- How can children contact a researcher if they wish to comment, question or complain?
- If children are not informed, how is this justified?

8. Consent

- As soon as they are old enough to understand, are children told that they can consent or refuse to take part in the research?
- Do they know that they can ask questions, perhaps talk to other people, and ask for time before they decide whether to consent?
- Do they know that if they refuse or withdraw from the research this will not be held against them in any way?
- How do the researchers help the children to know these things, and not to feel under pressure to give consent?
- How do they respect children who are too shy or upset to express their views freely?
- Are parents or guardians asked to give consent?
- What should researchers do if a child is keen to volunteer but the parents refuse?
- Is the consent written, oral or implied?
- If consent is given informally, how do the researchers ensure that each child's views are expressed and respected?
- If children are not asked for their consent, how is this justified?

9. Dissemination

- Does the research design allow enough time to report and publicise the research?
- Do the reports show the balance and range of evidence?
- Will the children and adults involved be sent short reports of the main findings?
- Will the research be reported in popular as well as academic and practitioner journals, so that the knowledge gained is shared more fairly through society?
- Can conferences or media reports be arranged to increase public information, and so encourage the public to believe that it is worthwhile to support research?
- Will the researchers meet practitioners to talk with them about practical ways of using the research findings?

10. Impact on children

- Besides the effects of the research on the children involved, how might the conclusions affect the larger groups of children?
- What models of childhood are assumed in the research?
  - Children as weak, vulnerable and dependent on adults? As immature, irrational and unreliable? As capable of being mature moral agents? As consumers?
- How do these models affect the methods of collecting and analysing data?
- Is the research reflexive, in that researchers critically discuss their own prejudices?
- Do they try to draw conclusions from the evidence or use the data to support their views?
- Do they aim to use positive images in reports and avoid stigmatising, discriminatory terms?
- Do they try to listen to children and report them on children's own terms, while remaining aware that children can only speak in public through channels designed by adults?
- Do they try to balance impartial research with respect for children's worth and dignity?

Appendix 2 Project information leaflets

Leaflet 1 summarises the ten topics questions into a format for children and young people to use and discuss. Leaflet 2 is an example of a project information leaflet for people aged from 3 years onwards.

Leaflet I

The following notes are written to be used directly with and by young people in two main ways:
- to photocopy and use in teaching and discussion groups (such as in citizenship and PHSE sessions)
- to draw on when writing project information leaflets for the young people who will be asked to take part.

Taking part in research: notes for young people

If you were asked to take part in some research, what would you say?

Here are some questions you might like to ask the researchers before you decide if you want to help them. There are notes about your rights. In the boxes are points to discuss, asking what you think about research.

Many young people are asked to help with research – surveys, interviews, market research, testing new services or teaching methods or commenting on their health care.

Asking about the research

What will happen to me?
Will there be a survey form to fill in, an interview, some kind of test, a diary to keep for a few days?
Does someone want to do a case study about me?
Will I be tape-recorded or filmed? What will it be like?

How long will it last?
Will I be asked to help once, or more often?
If so, how often and for how long?

Where will the research take place?

If I am asked questions -
Will they be about things I am happy to talk about?
Might some of the questions be very hard to answer?
Or about things that worry me, or that I'd rather not talk about?
Can I say 'no comment' or 'go on to the next question' to some of the
questions, if I want to? (Yes.)

What will happen to my answers?
And to any films, or notes, or other details about me?
Who else will see them? Would I mind if they saw them?
Do I want the researchers to make sure that no one else knows about
some, or all, of the details about me?
If so, how will they make sure that no one else knows?
By keeping my records locked up?
By not putting my details in their reports?
By reporting them, but making sure that no one else knows that they
are about me: such as by giving me a new name in their reports? Or
by not showing my face in their film? (see box 1).

Box 1. Famous or unknown?
You might like people to see your name in the research report or
on a TV film. If researchers use your ideas, it would be fair if
they thanked you in their reports. If they keep your name a
secret, that could mean that they get the credit for your ideas.

Yet if you are sure that no one else will know that it was you
talking, you might say more to the researcher about your private
views. You would also be safe from other people knowing too
much about you. If you want to go public, what would people

---

you know think? Might they laugh, or tease you, or be angry or upset?
Would you rather be famous or unknown, and for which kinds of views?

What is the research for?
Will it be used in a report, a book, a film, or somewhere else?
Who is doing the research, and why?
Who is paying for the research, and why?
What kinds of answers do they hope to find out?
Might the answers help me, or other young people?
Might the answers be unhelpful to us? (see box 2).

How many people will take part in the research?
Are there so many that some people's replies will be missed out of the reports or the film?
So might I be missed out?

Can one of my parents or a friend stay with me, if I want them to?
Can I take part in the research on my own, if I want to?

Box 2. Research that helps or harms?
What effect might the research have on you?
Will it be fun and worthwhile?
Might it bore you, or upset or worry you?
How might the research affect other young people?
Could it help to improve services for them, or show how mature they can be?
Or might it lead to worse services, or try to show that young people are stupid or selfish?

Will I be paid, or have a reward, for helping with the research?
If I have expenses, such as fares, will these be repaid to me?
If I need someone to come with me, will their fares be paid?
Will any payments be made on the day, or later? (see box 3).

> *Box 3. Rewards or bribes?*
> One view is that people should be paid for their time when they help with research. Another is that this could bribe them into doing research they would rather not do; it might be all right to give a badge or a T-shirt, but not money except for expenses. *What do you think?*

Why is the research being done with young people?
Research should not be done with young people, if it could be done just as well on adults (see box 4).
Is there a good reason why young people are involved?
Most researchers looking at young people's views have asked parents, teachers and other adults. Yet this kind of research cannot be done well without the help of young people. Is there a good reason why they are not involved?

> *Box 4. Children and young people last?*
> The rule that research should be done with adults first was made to protect young people from risk and harm, mainly of medical research. Adults are thought to be better at seeing problems in research and saying 'no'. But so far, little research has been done about young people's views on many aspects of their lives.
> *Do you think more or less research should be done with, and by, young people?*

Some research compares two or more groups of people.
Each group has a different 'treatment' (such as a way of teaching maths, classes on anti-smoking, or action against bullying). The aim is to see if one group does better than the others. These trials, which test a new treatment against older ones, aim to check which treatment is the best one. If you are asked to be in a trial, you might want to ask:
What kind of 'treatment' is each group having?
Do I mind being put into any of the groups?

In some trials, people cannot choose which group they will be in. This is decided by chance, like tossing a coin, or like the lottery balls. It is often done on a computer, and helps to make sure that treatments are compared in a fair way. If people are put into groups in this way, randomly, you may want to ask:

Do I mind my treatment being chosen by chance? (see box 5).

Box 5. Choice or chance?

If you decide to help with research, such as to test a new way of teaching maths, you may want to choose which group you will be in, not leave it to chance. Maybe you think that the new method looks very good, or that the old method is safer. Either way, you don't want to waste time; you want the best method. The point of having a trial is that no one knows which method is better. If they did, they wouldn't need to do the research. If you still feel unhappy about being put into a group you haven't chosen, that raises the question:

Do I mind having a teaching method or other 'treatment' that has not been tested to see if it is better?

Is there a leaflet I can keep about the research, to use while I'm thinking whether to take part, or to talk about with my friends?

Will I get a report or any news about the research when it is over?

The researchers should answer all your questions.

This should help you to decide if you think it is worth helping them. Doing so might not help you, but you might decide that it is worthwhile because it could help other people.

Do I have to say yes?
No. You can refuse to take part in research. No one should feel forced to agree (see box 6).

Do I have to decide at once?
If you are not sure about joining the research, ask for time to think about it. Most kinds of research can wait. You may want to talk to your family or friends before you decide.

What will happen if I say no?
You may worry about saying no, if your teacher or an adult caring for you is doing the research. They should make it clear that even if you refuse, they will go on giving you the best teaching or other care that they can.

Box 6. Whose right to decide?
There are no clear laws about consent to research. Some lawyers warn all medical researchers to ask for the parents' consent, until their child is 18. They should also ask young people as soon as they can understand. If even small children refuse, this should be taken very seriously. Many social researchers involve young people without asking them or, often, their parents. Some researchers ask parents to tell them a lot about their children, without asking for the child's consent or views. Some do secret research, such as watching people without telling them.

But standards are changing. More social researchers now agree that young people should be asked for their consent. They have the right to say no, even if their parents say yes, although young people seem to have less right to say yes if they want to help with research but their parents do not want them to.

Do you think you should decide with or without your parents' consent? Should your parents have your consent before they tell researchers about you?

Should young people be asked to sign consent forms as well, or instead of, their parents?
If there is a consent form, usually parents/guardians sign it.
Can I change my mind?
Perhaps you have agreed to take part in research, but later change your mind. You can opt out at any time, even if a consent form was signed. In a survey or interview, you can miss out some questions if you don't want to answer them all (see box 7). You can also say if you want a break, and then carry on again later. You do not have to say why you want to stop or miss out parts or change your mind. If you leave a project which you are not happy with, you could ask the researchers to give you any records they have about you, and not to use any of them in their reports.

Box 7. Questions about questions
Some research is very well planned, and the questions help people to give full and honest views. Other research is not so well planned. For example: a head teacher Ms Budget-Cuts was fed up with complaints about the school meals, and soggy chips. She sent survey forms round the school asking:
Do you think the chips are
good—, *very good*—, *very very good*—? *(please tick)*
Some surveys use questions like:
Do you think that kids hanging around the streets are:
a nuisance —, *a danger*———, *ought to be banned*—?
If you find that you are taking part in research like this, then you could start asking the questions:
Why is this research not well designed?
Why is it against young people?

How could research about young people improve if they have more say in how it is planned and carried out?

Leaflet 2
An example of an information leaflet for children and parents posted to them at home, by hospital staff

Living with diabetes
A research project
August – December 2003

This leaflet is for children aged 3-12 years
and their parents

Please will you help us with our research?

This leaflet gives some details about the project.
We have set out the questions you might want to ask, with our answers,
so you can talk about them together before you decide if you would like
to take part.

Please contact us, Katy or Priscilla, if you want more details and/or if you would like to join the project.

Katy Sutcliffe (phone and email)
Priscilla Alderson (phone and email)
(address)

Why is the research being done?

As you know, the way you care for yourself is vital to help you to keep healthy. But, so far, researchers have not asked children much about how they share in their own diabetes care.

We plan to listen to boys and girls, parents/carers, and health staff, and write reports about their views.

The aim is to help families and health care staff know more about the kinds of daily diabetes care that children and parents find work well.

What questions will the project ask?

- How do girls and boys with diabetes share in their daily health care, such as deciding what to eat and when?
- When are they old enough to do blood tests?
- Do you have any problems with diabetes? And, if so, how do you and your parents try to solve these?
- Do you remember when you first knew you had diabetes? Have there been any changes in your care since then? Would you like to make other changes?
- What do you find works well?
- How would you advise someone who has diabetes?

Who will be in the project?

Ten boys and girls at X —— Hospital and ten boys and girls at Y —— Hospital, and their parents.

The age groups are 3-6 and 10-12 years.

Dr B——— has chosen the children at your hospital to be asked to take part. He has not told us your names.

Do I have to take part?

You decide if you want to take part or not.
Even if you say 'yes', you can drop out at any time.
And you can tell us if you want to stop, or have a break.
If you don't want to answer some questions, just say 'pass'. You do not have to tell us anything unless you want to. And you don't have to give us a reason if you say 'no' or 'stop'. Whether you help us or not, you will still go on having just the same care at your hospital.

What will happen to me if I take part?

If you agree, one of us will meet you at your home, or at the clinic, to talk to you and your mother or father. We would like to tape-record you. You might play some games and talk with us for between 15 to 60 minutes. We will not look for right or wrong answers, it is your own views that matter. Later, we'll ask you to test a question booklet we will be writing for other children.

Could there be any problems for me if I take part?

We hope you will enjoy talking to us. A few people get upset when talking about their lives, and if they want to stop, we stop. We can put them in touch with someone to help them, if they wish. If you have any complaints about the project, please tell us, or Dr B———.

Will doing the research help me?

We hope you will like helping us. But our main aim is to write reports that will help very many families in the future. Maybe you too will find the reports useful.

Who will know if I am in the research, or what I have talked about?

Dr B——— will know if you are in the project, but we will not tell him or anyone else what you tell us.

The only time we might have to break this promise is if we think you or someone else might be at risk of being hurt. If so, we will talk to you first about the best thing to do.

We will keep our tapes and notes about you in a safe lockable place, and delete named details about you after the project.

When we write reports about your views, we will change your name, so no one will know you said that.

Will I know about the research results?

We will send you a short report in spring 2004, and longer reports too, if you want to see them.

The project is funded by a Social Science Research Unit grant. It was approved by X——— Hospital Research Ethics Committee, project number 405, and by Dr B———.

The researchers, Priscilla and Katy, do research and write reports and books about children's and parents' views on health care and education.

If you take part, please keep this leaflet with the copy of your consent form.

June 2003, leaflet version 1.

Thank you for reading this leaflet.

References

Access to Health Records Act Section 4 (2) (1990).

Age of Legal Capacity (Scotland) Act Section 2 (4) (1991).

Alderson, P (1993) *Children's consent to surgery*. Open University Press, Buckingham.

Alderson, P (1995) *Listening to children: children, ethics and social research*. Barnardo's, Barkingside.

Alderson, P (1998) Living with cystic fibrosis. *Association of CF Adults Magazine* (autumn): 8-9.

Alderson, P (1999) Did children change or the guidelines? *Bulletin of Medical Ethics* 150: 38-44.

Alderson, P (2000) Children as researchers. In Christensen, P, James, A (eds) *Research with children*. Routledge Falmer, London.

Alderson, P (2000a) School students' views on school councils and daily life at school. *Children & Society* 14: 121-134.

Alderson, P, Goodey, C (1998) *Enabling education: Experiences in ordinary and special schools*. Tufnell, London.

Alderson, P, Montgomery, M (1996) *Health care choices: making decisions with children*. IPPR, London.

Beauchamp, T, Childress, J (2000) *Principles of biomedical ethics*. Oxford University Press, New York.

Beresford, B (1997) *Personal accounts: involving disabled children in research*. The Stationery Office, London.

BMA – British Medical Association (2001) *Consent, rights and choices in health care for children and young people.* BMA, London.

Borland, M, Hill, M, Laybourn, A, Stafford, A (2001) *Improving Consultation with Children and Young People in Relevant Aspects of Policy-making and Legislation in Scotland.* The Scottish Parliament, Edinburgh.

Boyden, J, Ennew, J (eds) (1997) *Children in Focus – a manual for participatory research with children.* Radda Barnen, Stockholm.

Bradley, B (1989) *Visions of infancy.* Polity, Cambridge.

Brazier, M, Lobjoit, M (1991) *Protecting the vulnerable: autonomy and consent in health care.* Routledge, London.

Bricher, G (2001) *'If you want to know about it just ask': exploring disabled young people's experiences of health and health care.* Unpublished PhD, University of South Australia, Adelaide.

British Education Research Association (1992) *Ethical Guidelines.* BERA, Slough.

BPS – British Psychological Society (1991) *Revised ethical principles for constructing research with human participants.* BPS, Leicester.

BPS – British Psychological Society (2000) *A Code of Conduct for Psychologists.* BPS, Leicester.

Brooker, E (2002) *Starting school: young children learning cultures.* Open University Press, Buckingham.

Brunton, G, Harden, A, Rees, R, Kavanagh, J, Oliver, S, Oakley, A (2003) *Children and physical activity: a systematic review of barriers and facilitators.* EPPI-Centre, Social Science Research Unit, Institute of Education, University of London.

British Sociological Association (1993, 2003) *Guidelines for good professional conduct and statement of ethical practice; Statement of Ethical Practice*. BSA, Durham. www.britsoc.co.uk. Accessed 18 February 2004.

Cambridge, P (1993) Taking account of user choice in community care. In Alderson, P (ed) *Disabled people and consent to medical treatment and research*. SSRU Institute of Education, London.

Candappa, M (2002) Human rights and refugee children in the UK. In Franklin, B (ed) *The new handbook of children's rights*. Routledge Falmer, London.

Children Act (England and Wales) (1989) Part V, 43, (8). HMSO, London.

Code of Practice Pursuant to Section 118(4) of the Mental Health Act 1983 (1990). HMSO, London.

Children in Scotland (2002) *Research/Consultation Guidelines*. CiS, Edinburgh.

Children's Forum (2002) A world fit for us, *Children's Rights Information Network News* 16: 12.

Christensen, P, James, A (eds) (2000) *Research with children. Perspectives and practices*. Routledge/Falmer, London.

Clark, A, Moss, P (2001) *Listening to young children. The Mosaic Approach*. National Children's Bureau/Joseph Rowntree Foundation, London.

Clarke-Jones, L in Alderson, P, Clarke-Jones, L, Schaumberg, H (2002) *Notes towards an evaluation of The Office of Children's Rights Commissioner for London: Phase 1. 2000-2001*. End of project report to funders.

Cleves School, Alderson, P (ed) (1999) *Learning and Inclusion: the Cleves School Experience.* David Fulton, London.

Cockburn, T, Kenny, S, Webb, M (1997) *Moss Side Youth Audit: phase 2, indicative findings in employment and training.* Manchester City Council and Manchester Metropolitan University, Manchester.

Code of Practice Pursuant to Section 118 (4) of the Mental Health Act 1983 (1990). HMSO, London.

Cooter, R (ed) (1992) *In the name of the child: health and welfare 1880-1940.* Routledge, London.

Davis, J (1998) Understanding the meanings of children: a reflexive process, *Children & Society*, 12 (5): 325-335.

Davis, J, Watson, N, Cunningham Burley, S (2000) Learning the lives of disabled children: developing a reflexive approach. In Christensen P, James, A (eds) *Research with children.* Routledge/Falmer, London.

Davis, J, Hogan, J (2003) Research with children: ethnography, participation, disability, self-empowerment. Paper to ESRC Disability Seminar Series: *From Theory to Practice: Implementing the social model of disability.*

Davis, J, Hogan, J (2003a) *Diversity and difference: Consultation and involvement of disabled children and young people in Liverpool.* Liverpool Bureau/The Children's Society, Liverpool.

Denning, LJ in *Hewer v Bryant* [1970] 1 QB 357, 369.

DfES – Department for Education and Skills (2001) *Code of Practice concerning special educational needs.* London: DfES, paragraphs 33: 15-16.

DfES – Department for Education and Skills (2001a) *Core principles for the involvement of children and young people.* Children and Young People's Unit, London.

DfES – Department for Education and Skills (2003) *Every Child Matters*. Consultation Paper. DfES, London.

DoH – Department of Health (1990) *Patient consent to examination or treatment* Health Circular (90)22.

DoH – Department of Health (2001) *Research governance framework for health and social care*. Department of Health, London.

DoH – Department of Health (2001a) *Consent – what you have a right to expect: a guide for parents*. Department of Health, London.

Donnelly, M (2003) *Consulting children and young people in Liverpool*. Liverpool City Council, Liverpool.

Douglas, G (1992) Limiting Gillick. *Bulletin of Medical Ethics* 75: 34-5.

Dunn, J (1998) Young children's understanding of other people: evidence from observations within the family. In Woodhead, M, Faulkner, D, Littleton, K (eds) *Cultural worlds of early childhood*. Routledge, London.

Ekstedt, J, Nomura, B (2002) A place at the top table in South America, *Children's Rights Information Network News* 16: 15-16.

ESRC – Economic and Social Research Council *Children 5-16 Research Programme*. www.hull.ac.uk/children5to16programme/. Accessed 20 February 2004.

EU – European Union, RESPECT. www.respectproject.org.

European Clinical Trials Directive: the Medicines for Human Use (Clinical Trials) Regulations, implemented in the UK 2004. www.corec.org.uk. Accessed 18 May 2004.

Faden, R, Beauchamp, T (1986) *A history and theory of informed consent*. Oxford University Press, New York.

Finch, J (1984) 'It's great to have someone to talk to': ethics and politics of interviewing women. In Bell, C, Roberts, H (eds) *Social researching: politics, problems, practice*. Routledge, London.

France, A (2000) *Youth researching youth: the Triumph and Success peer research project*. NGA/JRF, Leicester.

Franklin, B (ed) (2002) *The new handbook of children's rights*. Routledge/Falmer, London.

Fraser, S, Lewis, V, Ding, S, Kellett, M, Robinson, C (eds) (2004) *Doing research with children and young people*. Sage/Open University, London.

Galloway, D, Armstrong, D, Tomlinson, S (1994) *The assessment of special educational needs: whose problem?* Longman, London.

Gillick v West Norfolk & Wisbech AHA (1985) 1 All ER.

Gillon, R (ed) (1986) *Philosophical medical ethics*. Wiley, Chichester.

Gordon, D, Adelman, L, Ashworth, K, Bradshaw, J, Levitas, R, Middleton, S, Pantazis, C, Patsios, D, Payne, S, Townsend, P, Williams, J (2000) *Poverty and social exclusion in Britain*. Joseph Rowntree Foundation, York.

Grodin, M A, Glantz, L H (1994) *Children as research subjects: science ethics and law*. Oxford University Press, New York.

Hastings Center (1999) *Empirical Research on Informed Consent*, Hastings Center Report Special Supplement 29, 1: S1-S42.

Hart, R (1992) *Children's participation: from tokenism to citizenship*. UNICEF, Paris.

Hart, R, Lansdown, G (2002) Changing world opens door to children. *CRIN News* 16: 9-11.

Hill, M (2004) Ethical considerations in researching children's experiences. In Greene, S and Hogan, D M (eds) *Researching children's experiences*. Sage, London.

Hood, S (2002) *The State of London's Children*. Office of the Children's Rights Commissioner for London, National Children's Bureau, London.

Howarth, R and Hopscotch Asian Women's Centre (1997) '*If we don't play now, when can we?*' Hopscotch Asian Women's Centre, London.

Human Rights Act (1998). The Stationery Office, London.

James, A, Prout, A (eds) (1997) *Constructing and reconstructing childhood*. Falmer, London.

Karkara, R, O'Kane, C (2002) Young citizens for a new era in South and central Asia, *Children's Rights Information Network News*, 16: 13-4.

Katz, A (ed), (2002) *Parenting Under Pressure: Prison*. Young Voice, London.

Kellett, M, Nind, M (2001) Ethics in quasi-experimental research on people with severe learning difficulties: dilemmas and compromises, *British Journal of Learning Difficulties*, 29: 51-5.

Kellett, M, with Ruth Forrest (aged 10), Naomi Dent (aged 10) Simon Ward (aged 10) (2004) Just teach us the skills please, we'll do the rest: empowering 10-year-olds as active researchers. *Children & Society* Early View. www3.interscience.wiley.com. Accessed 18 February 2004.

Kennedy, I (1988) *Treat me right*. Clarendon Press, Oxford.

Kennedy, I (2001) *The Report of the Independent Inquiries into Paediatric Cardiac Services at the Royal Brompton Hospital and Harefield Hospital*. The Stationery Office, London.

Kessel, R (1989) (Mis)Understanding Cleveland: foundational issues and the sexual abuse of children. *Paediatric and perinatal epidemiology*, 3: 347-52.

King, M, Yuille, J, (1987) Suggestibility and the child witness. In Ceci, S, Toglia, M, Ross, D (eds) *Children's eyewitness memory*. Springer-Verlag, New York. Quoted in Spencer, J, Flin, R (1990) *The evidence of children: the law and psychology*. Blackstone Press, London.

Kingsman, S (1992) Periods of anxiety. *Health Education*, May.

Kirby, P, Lanyon, C, Cronin, K, Sinclair, R (2003) *Building a culture of participation: involving children and young people in policy, service planning, delivery and evaluation*. DfES, London.

Lancaster, P, Broadbent, V (2003) *Listening to young children training pack*. Open University Press/McGraw Hill, London.

Lawson, E (1991) Are Gillick rights under threat? *Childright*, 80: 17-21.

Lewis, A (2002) Accessing, through research interviews, the views of children with difficulties in learning. *Support for Learning* 17, 3: 110-6.

Lewis, J (2002) Research and development in social care: governance and good practice. *Research Policy and Planning* 20, 1:3-9.

Liebel, M (2004) *A will of their own. Cross-cultural perspectives on working children*. Zed Press, London.

MacDougall, H (2003) *'It's about respect'. Focus groups with young people on their views about research ethics*. Barnardo's, Barkingside.

Mayall, B (2002) *Towards a sociology for childhood*. Routledge/Falmer, London.

Mayall, B, Hood, S (2001) Breaking Barriers – Provision and Participation in an Out-of-School Centre, *Children & Society*, 15: 70-81.

Mayor of London (2004) *Towards a child-friendly London: The Mayor's Draft Children and Young People's Strategy.* GLA, London.

McNeish, D (1999) *From rhetoric to reality: participatory approaches to health promotion with young people.* London, HEA.

Melville, R, Urquhart, R (2002) *Partners in ethical dilemmas: on academics and practitioners collaborating.* Uniting Care Burnside, Sydney.

Miller, J (1996) *Never too young: how young children can take responsibility and make decisions. A handbook for early years workers.* National Early Years Network and Save the Children, London.

Miller, J (1998) 'We didn't mean to do that!' *Co-ordinate,* 67: 5-6.

Montgomery, J (1992) Parents and children in dispute: who has the final word? *Journal of Child Law.* April: 85-9.

Montgomery, J (1997) *Health care law.* Oxford University Press, Oxford.

Morris, J (1998) *Don't leave us out! Involving disabled children and young people with communication impairments.* Joseph Rowntree Foundation, York.

Morrow, V (1998) 'If you were a teacher, it would be harder to talk to you': reflections on qualitative research with children in school. *International Journal of Social Research Methodology: theory and practice,* 1, 4: 297-313.

Morrow, V (2001) Using qualitative methods to elicit young people's perspectives on their environments: some ideas for community health initiatives. *Health Education Research: Theory and Practice,* 16, 3: 255-68.

Morrow, V, Richards, M (1996) The ethics of social research with children: an overview. *Children & Society,* 10: 90-105.

Murray, K (1988) *Evidence from Children*. Scottish Law Commission, Edinburgh.

NCB – National Children's Bureau (2003) *Guidelines for Research*. NCB, London. www.ncb.org.uk/ourwork/research_guidelines.pdf. Accessed 18 February 2004.

NCH – National Children's Homes (2001a) *Participating in good practice: a resource pack to support user participation in NCH projects*. NCH, London.

NCH (2001b) *Positive image: NCH photographic guidelines*. NCH, London.

Nicholson, R (ed) (1986) *Medical research with children: ethics, law and practice*. Oxford University Press, Oxford.

Noyes, J (1999) *The voices and choices of children on long-term ventilation. Their health and social care, and education*. Stationery Office, London.

Nuffield – Nuffield Council on Bioethics (1999) *The ethics of clinical research in developing countries*. Nuffield Foundation, London.

Nuremberg Code (1947). ohsr.od.nih.gov/guidelines/nuremberg.html. Accessed 23 June 2004.

Oakley, A, Wiggins, M, Turner, H, Rajan, L, Barker, M (2003) Including culturally diverse samples in health research: a case study of an urban trial of social support. *Ethnicity and Health* 8, 1: 29-39.

OCRCL – Office of the Children's Rights Commission for London (2001) *Sort it out!* Report of survey of 3,000 young Londoners. OCRCL, London.

Office of the Children's Rights Commission for London (2002a) *Advisory Board Handbook*. OCRCL, London.

Office of the Children's Rights Commission for London (2002b) *Children & young people's participation in decision-making in London.* OCRCL, London.

O'Kane, C (2000) The development of participatory techniques: facilitating children's views about decisions which affect them. In Christensen, P, James, A (eds) *Research with children.* Routledge Falmer, London.

Osler, A, Street, C, Lall, M, Vincent, K (2002) *Not a problem? Girls and school exclusion.* Joseph Rowntree Foundation/National Children's Bureau, London.

Oswin, M (1971) *The empty hours.* Penguin, Harmondsworth.

Plant, R (1992) Citizenship in rights and welfare. In Coote, A (ed) *The welfare of citizens.* IPPR, London.

Porter, J, Lewis, A (2001) Methodological issues in interviewing children and young people with learning difficulties. *ESRC Briefing Paper.* Birmingham University: School of Education.

Prendergast, S (1994) *'This is the time to grow up': girl's experiences of menstruation in school.* Family Planning Association, London.

Prendergast, S (1995) 'With gender on my mind': menstruation and embodiment at adolescence' in Holland, J, Blair, M (eds) *Debates and issues in feminist research and pedagogy.* Open University Press, Buckingham.

Punch, S (2002) Research with children: the same or different from research with adults? *Childhood,* 9 3: 321-341.

Qvortrup, J, Bardy, M, Sgritta, G, Wintersberger, H (1994) (eds) *Childhood matters. Social theory, practice and politics.* Avebury, Aldershot.

Redfern, M (2001) *The Royal Liverpool Children's Hospital Inquiry Report.* The Stationery Office, London.

Robertson, J, Robertson, J (1989) *Separation and the very young.* Free Association Books, London.

RCPCH – Royal College of Paediatrics and Child Health (2000) Guidelines for the ethical conduct of medical research involving children. *Archives of Disease in Childhood* 82: 177-182.

RCP – Royal College of Physicians (1986) *Research on healthy volunteers.* RCP, London.

RCP – Royal College of Physicians (1990) *Guidelines on the practice of ethics committees in medical research involving human subjects.* RCP, London.

RCP – Royal College of Physicians (1990a) *Research involving patients.* RCP, London.

Samaritans (2002) *Media Guidelines: Portrayals of suicide.* Samaritans, Surrey.

Save the Children (1997) *Learning from experience: participatory approaches in SCF.* Save the Children, London.

Save the Children (1999) *We have rights OK!* Save the Children, London.

Scottish Law Commission (1988) *The evidence of children and other potentially vulnerable witnesses.* Scottish Law Commission, Edinburgh.

Sharav, V (2003) Children in clinical research: a conflict of moral values. *American Journal of Bioethics* 3,1: 1-99.

Smart, C, Neale, B, Wade, A (2001) *The changing experiences of childhood: families and divorce.* Polity, Cambridge.

Smith, F, Barker, J (1999) *Child Centred After School and Holiday Care*. Final report to the ESRC.

Smith, F, Barker, J (2002) School's out. In Edwards, R (ed) *Children, home and school*. Routledge/Falmer, London.

Solberg, A (1997) Negotiating childhood. In James, A, Prout, A (eds) *Constructing and reconstructing childhood*. Falmer Press, Basingstoke.

Stainton Rogers, R, Stainton Rogers, W (1992) *Stories of Childhood: Shifting Agendas in Child Concern*. Harvester, Hemel Hempstead.

Swift, A (1997) *Children for social change: education for citizenship of street and working children in Brazil*. Educational Heretics, Nottingham.

Thomas, N, O'Kane, C (1998) The ethics of participatory research with children, *Children & Society* 12, 5, 336-48.

United Nations (1989) *Convention on the Rights of the Child*. UN, New York.

United Nations Committee on the Rights of the Child (1995, 2003) *Consideration of Reports Submitted by States Parties Under Article 44 of the Convention, Concluding Observations: United Kingdom of Great Britain and Northern Ireland*. United Nations, Geneva.

van Beers, H (2002) Pushing the participation agenda – experiences from Africa, *Children's Rights Information Network News*, 16: 19-20.

Vernon, T (1980) *Gobbledegook*. NCC, London.

Walter, I, Nutley, S, Percy-Smith, J, McNeish, D, Frost, S (2004) *Improving the use of research in social care practice*, Knowledge Review 7. SCIE, London.

Ward, L (1997) *Seen and heard: involving disabled children and young people in research and development projects.* Joseph Rowntree Foundation, York.

Wendler, D, Rackoff, J, Emanuel, E, Grady, G (2002) Commentary: the ethics of paying for children's participation in research. *Journal of Pediatrics*, 141, 2:166-71.

Willow, C (1997) *Hear! Hear! Promoting children's and young people's democratic participation in government.* Local Government Information Unit, London.

Woodhead, M, Faulkner, D (2000) Subjects, objects or participants? Dilemmas of psychological research with children. In Christensen, P, James, A (eds) *Research with children.* Routledge/Falmer, London.

WMA – World Medical Association. (2000/1964) *Declaration of Helsinki.* World Medical Association, Fernay-Voltaire.

Index

abstracts 119
acknowledgement 52, 92
assent 97

benefit 25, 36-7
    harm-benefit analysis 28, 29, 30,
    31, 37-40
bioethics 27
British Sociological Association (BSA)
43-4, 54

caution 26-8
Central Office for Research Ethics
Committees 79
Children in Scotland 61, 72-3
children and young people 9
    consent 98-100
    and ethical standards 12, 26
    exclusion from research 60-2
    impact of research 125-8, 142
    new approaches to research 10-11
    research ethics 27, 31
    as researchers 64-6
    rights 10
    theories 22
confidence 26-8
confidentiality 43-6, 121, 138-9
    personal data 51-2
    respecting 47-9
consent 26-7, 35, 95-6, 110, 132, 141
    children and young people 98-100
    competence 102-5
    law 98
    levels of involvement 105-6
    meaning 96-7
    parents 100-1
    requesting and respecting 106-10
contracts 70-1
Convention on the Rights of the
Child 10, 65, 105, 117, 127

COREC 79
covert research 109

Data Protection Act 1998 43, 48, 50-1
Declaration of Helsinki 26-8, 39-40, 96
dissemination 115-16, 141
    critical readers and viewers 123-4
    and implementation 116-18
    and mass media 121-2
    problems and solutions 118-20
Diversity and Difference Group 62,
116-17
duty 25, 28-9, 30, 31

emotions 55, 56
ESRC (Economic and Social
Research Council) 49
ethics *see* research ethics
Every child matters (DfES) 10
exclusions 60-2, 64

Findings (Joseph Rowntree
Foundation) 119
funding 69-73, 139

Gillick case 97, 99, 100, 105
group sessions 53

harm 26, 35-6, 50, 96, 135
harm-benefit analysis 28, 29, 30, 31,
37-40
Hart, R 100
Helsinki 26-8, 39-40, 96

implementation 116-18, 126
inclusion 60-3, 64
information 83, 140
    two-way 89-93

information leaflets 83-7, 143-53
  languages 88-9
  layout 87-8
informed consent 26-7, 35, 98
  see also consent
insiders 13, 14-15
internet 54-5
interviews 52-4

Joseph Rowntree Foundation 119

Lansdown, G 100
local research ethics committees
(LRECs) 11, 78, 98
London 117-18

mass media 119, 121-2
medical ethics 11, 25-8, 60
methods 16, 21-2, 24-5
Mosaic Approach 24-5

National Children's Bureau 70-1, 128
Nuremberg Code 26, 71

Office of Children's Rights
Commissioner for London (OCRCL)
117-18
online consultations 54-5
opt-in research 46-7
opt-out research 46-7
outsiders 14

parents, consent 100-1
participants 9, 104
  payments 71-3
participation 123-4, 135
participatory research 24-5, 64-5, 105-
6, 131
payments 71-3
personal data 50-2
power 55, 56

privacy 43, 138-9
  opt-in or opt-out research 46-7
  respecting 47-9
  rights 49-52
protection 50, 62-3, 123-4, 135
provision 50, 123-4

reporting back 90-3
research
  consent 95-110, 141
  dissemination 115-24, 141
  ethics frameworks 28-31
  framing 59-62
  funding 69-73, 139
  harms and benefits 35-40, 137-8
  impact on children 125-8, 142
  information leaflets 83-9, 140, 143-
53
  methods 24-5
  newer approaches 10-11
  privacy and confidentiality 43-57,
138-9
  purpose and methods 21-2, 137
  review 75-80, 140
  selection, inclusion and
participation 59-66, 139
  theories 22
  viewpoints 23-4
research ethics 11-13
  growing awareness 25-8
  practical questions 137-42
  relationships, power and emotions
55-7
  respect, inclusion and protection
62-3
  and social exclusion 64
  uncertainty 32-3
  ways forward 131
research ethics committees (RECs)
11, 27, 75, 76-80, 132-4
research relationships 52-3, 55, 56
research subjects *see* participants

researchers 9, 15
    children and young people 64-6
respect 26, 47-9
    consent 95-6, 101, 105-10
    inclusion and protection 62-3
    two-way information 89-90
reviews 75-6, 132, 140
    research ethics committees 76-80
rights 10, 43
    confidentiality 43-6
    ethics frameworks 28, 29, 30, 31
    and internet 54-5
    privacy 46-7, 49-52
    research ethics 26
risk-benefit assessments 37-40
risk probability 40
risk severity 40
risks 39-40

social exclusion 64
social research 9
    ethics authorities 132-4
    ways forward 131-2
standpoints 23-4

T v L 44-6
theories 22

uncertainty 32-3
United Nations
    Committee on the Rights of the
    Child 127
    Convention on the Rights of the
    Child (UNCRC) 10, 65, 105, 117,
    127
utilitarianism 29

young people *see* children and young
people
Young Voice 89-90, 121-2